# Teaching ESL/EFL Reading and Writing

Using a framework based on principles of teaching and learning, this guide for teachers and teacher trainees provides a wealth of suggestions for helping learners at all levels of proficiency develop their reading and writing skills and fluency. By following these suggestions, which are organized around four strands—meaning-focused input, meaning-focused output, language-focused learning, and fluency development—teachers will be able to design and present a balanced program for their students.

*Teaching ESL/EFL Reading and Writing*, and its companion text, *Teaching ESL/EFL Listening and Speaking*, are similar in format and the kinds of topics covered, but do not need to be used together. Drawing on research and theory in applied linguistics, their focus is strongly hands-on, featuring

- easily applied principles,
- a large number of useful teaching techniques, and
- guidelines for testing and monitoring.

All Certificate, Diploma, Masters and Doctoral courses for teachers of English as a second or foreign language include a teaching methods component. The texts are designed for and have been field tested in such programs.

**I. S. P. Nation** is Professor of Applied Linguistics in the School of Linguistics and Applied Language Studies at Victoria University in Wellington, New Zealand.

## ESL & Applied Linguistics Professional Series
*Eli Hinkel, Series Editor*

Visit www.routledgeeducation.com for additional information on titles in the ESL & Applied Linguistics Professional Series

# Teaching ESL/EFL Reading and Writing

I. S. P. Nation

Routledge
Taylor & Francis Group

NEW YORK AND LONDON

First published 2009
by Routledge
711 Third Avenue, New York, NY 10017

Simultaneously published in the UK
by Routledge
2 Park Square, Milton Park, Abingdon, Oxon OX14 4RN

*Routledge is an imprint of the Taylor & Francis Group, an informa business*

© 2009 Routledge, Taylor & Francis

Typeset in Minion by
RefineCatch Limited, Bungay, Suffolk

*Library of Congress Cataloging-in-Publication Data*
Nation, I. S. P.
  Teaching ESL/EFL reading and writing / I. S. P. Nation.
    p. cm.—(ESL & applied linguistics professional series)
  Includes bibliographical references.
    1. English language—Study and teaching—Foreign speakers.   2. English language—Rhetoric—Study and teaching.   3. English teachers—Training of.   I. Title.
  PE1128.A2N345 2008
  428.2′4—dc22                                                          2008011762

ISBN10: 0–415–98967–1 (hbk)
ISBN10: 0–415–98968–X (pbk)
ISBN10: 0–203–89164–3 (ebk)

ISBN13: 978–0–415–98967–1 (hbk)
ISBN13: 978–0–415–98968–8 (pbk)
ISBN13: 978–0–203–89164–3 (ebk)

Printed in Canada

# Contents

# Preface

This book (and its companion book *Teaching ESL/EFL Listening and Speaking*) is intended for teachers of English as a second or foreign language. It can be used both for experienced teachers and for teachers in training. In its earlier forms this book has been used on graduate diploma and Masters level courses, and with teachers in training.

The book has two major features. First, it has a strong practical emphasis—around one hundred teaching techniques are described in the book. Second, it tries to provide a balanced programme for developing the skills of reading and writing. It does this by using a framework called the four strands. These are called strands because they run through the whole course. They are the strands of meaning-focused input, meaning-focused output, language-focused learning, and fluency development. In a well-balanced language programme covering the four skills of listening, speaking, reading, and writing, each of the four strands should have roughly equal amounts of time. The organisation of the book largely reflects these four strands.

I have attempted to write the book using clear and simple language. Wherever possible, technical terms have been avoided. However, in a few cases, with terms such as *phonics*, *topic type*, and *extensive reading*, technical terms have been used and explained in the text. This book thus does not require any previous knowledge of second language acquisition theory or language teaching methodology.

Chapter 1 compares first and second language reading. The first six chapters look at reading, and the last four at writing. Chapters 2 and 3 focus on beginning reading. Special attention is given to phonics and there is a very useful related appendix of spelling–sound correspondences. Chapters 4 and 5 look at extensive reading and fluency. Chapter 6 looks at assessing reading, paying particular attention to the reasons for testing. Chapter 7 presents a range of ways for supporting writing and Chapter 8 examines the writing process. Chapter 9 has relevance for both reading and writing. It looks at topic types which describe the kinds of information contained in different kinds of texts. Chapter 10 examines a range of ways that can be used to respond to written work.

As a result of working through this book, teachers should be able to design a well-balanced reading and writing course which provides a good range of opportunities for learning. The teacher's most important job is to plan so that the learners are learning useful things, so that the best conditions for learning occur, and so that they are getting a balance of learning opportunities. This book should help teachers do this.

Wherever possible, the ideas in this book are research based. This is reflected in the principles which are described at the end of Chapter 1 and which are referred to throughout the book. The idea which lies behind these principles is that it is not a wise idea to follow closely a particular method of language teaching, such as communicative language teaching or the direct method. It is much more sensible to draw, where possible, on research-based principles which can be adapted or discarded as new research evidence becomes available.

There are many people who should be thanked for their help in the production of this book. Eli Hinkel gave me a great deal of very supportive encouragement to get me to offer the book for publication. Mary Hillemeier and Naomi Silverman of Taylor & Francis were similarly enthusiastic and took away a lot of the burden of publication. The reviewers of the book before it was published provided many helpful and frank comments which led me to see the book through others' eyes. I am very grateful for this. I would like to take this opportunity to acknowledge my own teachers, H.V. George and Helen Barnard, who were also my mentors and colleagues. They were both great teachers and wonderful people, and their legacy is reflected in the very large number of grateful students who remember and apply their teaching.

Both this book and its companion volume, *Teaching ESL/EFL Listening and Speaking*, were largely written and used in teacher training courses before they were offered for publication. There was thus a lot of input from the teachers who were studying on these courses.

I would feel that the book's purpose has been achieved if, as a result of reading it, teachers learn some new techniques and activities, understand why these activities are used, and see how they fit into the larger programme.

Teaching English and training teachers of English are challenging but very rewarding professions. I have been involved in them for a very long time and they have given me a great deal of enjoyment. I hope that this enjoyment is apparent in the book and that it will help readers gain similar enjoyment.

# CHAPTER 1

# Learning to Read in Another Language

In the companion volume to this one, *Teaching ESL/EFL Listening and Speaking* (Nation and Newton, 2009), the four strands of a language course are described. The basic idea behind the four strands is that, in a well-balanced language course, equal time is given to each of the four strands of meaning-focused input, meaning-focused output, language-focused learning, and fluency development. Meaning-focused input involves getting input through listening and reading where the learners' focus is on understanding the message and where only a small proportion of language features are outside the learners' present level of proficiency. In a reading and writing programme, extensive reading is likely to be the major source of meaning-focused input.

Meaning-focused output involves the learners producing language through speaking and writing where the learners' focus is on others understanding the message. Meaning-focused output occurs when learners write essays and assignments, when they write letters, when they write a diary, when they send email and text messages to each other, and when they write about their experience.

Language-focused learning involves deliberate attention to language features both in the context of meaning-focused input and meaning-focused output, and in decontextualised learning and teaching. In the reading and writing programme, language-focused learning occurs in intensive reading, when learners consult dictionaries in reading and writing, when they get language-focused feedback on their writing, when they deliberately learn new vocabulary for receptive or productive use, when they practise spelling, when they concentrate on learning to write or form written letters of the alphabet, and when they study grammar and discourse features. There are lots of ways of making language-focused learning a part of the course, but a teacher needs to be careful that this does not take up more than 25 percent of the total course time.

Fluency development is often neglected in courses, partly because teachers and learners feel that they should always be learning something new. Fluency development involves making the best use of what is already known. The best-known kind of fluency development is speed reading where learners focus on increasing their reading speed while still maintaining good comprehension. For speed reading courses to work well with learners of English as a second or foreign language, the reading material needs to be well within the learners' level of proficiency. There should be little or no unknown vocabulary or grammatical features in the speed reading texts. Writing fluency also needs to get attention in a well-balanced course, especially where learners need to sit a written test as part of academic study and where they have to write under time pressure.

These four strands of meaning-focused input, meaning-focused output, language-focused learning, and fluency development need to take up roughly equal time in a language course. As we shall see, there are many ways of getting this balance, and the way this is done depends on local conditions, teacher preferences, the way the classes are divided up and scheduled, and timetabling constraints. What is important is that over a period of time probably no greater than a month or two, there is a roughly equal amount of time given to each of these four strands, and that the necessary conditions exist for the strands to occur. In this book, this idea of the four strands will be applied to goals as diverse as learning to spell, learning to write, and becoming fluent in reading.

The first six chapters of this book focus largely on reading, and the next four on writing, although links will be made between these skills and also with the skills of listening and speaking. This is a lot to cover in such a small number of chapters, so this book should be seen as a practical overview of what can be done in the reading and writing programme. There are long traditions of research into reading and writing and this research is drawn on particularly to justify certain teaching and learning procedures.

Let us now look at a beginner learning to read.

## Learning to Read in the First Language

People learn to read their first language in a wide variety of circumstances. The following description is of a fortunate child in a fortunate country where reading is well prepared for and well taught. An excellent account of the teaching of reading to native speakers in New Zealand can be found in Smith and Elley (1997).

Children are prepared for reading at an early age by listening to stories, being read to, and interacting with adults and others about the stories they hear. This is done not with the main purpose of preparing a child for reading but as a way that parents and others interact with, show affection for, and entertain and educate children. The interaction involves asking questions about what is going to happen in the story, getting the child to complete sentences in a known story, talking about the interesting and scary parts of the story, and generally having fun.

When native-speaking children start to learn to read, they already have a large vocabulary of several thousand words which includes most of the words they will meet in early reading. They also have good control of the grammar of the language, have a lot of knowledge about books and reading conventions, and have had many many stories read to them. They are very keen to learn how to read.

They begin formal schooling at the age of about five or six. The teacher and learners work with books that are interesting, are well illustrated, use language that is close to spoken language, and are not too long. The texts contain a lot of repetition, and are often very predictable but in an interesting way.

The techniques used to teach reading are largely meaning-focused. That is, they give primary attention to understanding and enjoying the story. They include shared reading, guided reading and independent reading. A small amount of attention may be given to phonological awareness and phonics but this is in the context of enjoying the story and only takes a very small amount of time. Let us now look at the typical techniques used to teach reading to young native speakers.

*Shared Reading*

The learners gather around the teacher and the teacher reads a story to the learners from a very large blown-up book while showing them the pictures and the written words. The teacher involves the learners in the reading by asking them what they think will happen next and getting them to comment on the story. Where they can, the learners read the words aloud together. The procedure is an attempt to make the shared book activity like a parent reading a child a bedtime story.

The learners are asked to choose what blown-up book they want read to them and the same book may be used in the shared book activity on several occasions. In the later readings, the learners are expected to join in the reading much more. At other times, learners can take the small version of the blown-up book and read it individually or in pairs. After a reading, the learners draw, write, act out the story or study some of the language in the story.

The **shared book** activity is a very popular reading activity in New Zealand pre-schools and primary schools. It was developed by a New Zealander, Don Holdaway, and is such a normal part of a primary teacher's repertoire that publishers now print blown-up book versions of popular children's books.

The purpose of the shared book activity is to get the learners to see the fun element in reading. In the activity, this fun comes from the interesting story, the interaction between the teacher and the learners in predicting and commenting on the story, and the rereading of favourite stories.

Teachers can make blown-up books. Although a blown-up book takes some time to make, it will be used and re-used and well repays the effort of making it or the cost of buying it. The books also make attractive displays in the classroom. The shared book activity was used in one of the experimental groups in the Elley and Mangubhai (1981) Book Flood experiment. Blown-up books can be bought from the following publishers: Nelson Price Milburn (http://www.newhouse.co.nz/), Giltedge Publishing (http://www.giltedgepublishing.co.nz/). Titles include *Where Do Monsters Live?*; *Bears, Bears Everywhere*; *Mr Noisy*; *What Do You See?*; *Pirate Pete*; *William's Wet Week*; *The Sunflower Tree*.

*Guided Reading*

**Guided reading** can be done silently or with a child reading aloud to a friend, parent or teacher. Before the reading the learner and teacher talk about the book. Research by Wong and McNaughton (1980) showed that for the learner they studied, pre-reading discussion resulted in a greater percentage of words initially correct, and a greater percentage of errors self-corrected. The teacher and the learner look at the title of the book and make sure that all the words in the title are known. Then they talk about the pictures in the story and make predictions about what might happen in the story and talk about any knowledge the learner already has about the topic. Important words in the story are talked about but need not be pointed to in their written form. So, before the learner actually starts to read the story, the ideas and important words in the story are talked about and clarified. Then the learner begins to read.

If the learner is reading aloud to the teacher, then it is good to use the pause, prompt, praise procedure (Glynn et al., 1989; Smith and Elley, 1997: 134–136). This means that when the learner starts to struggle over a word the teacher does not rush in with the answer but pauses for the learner to have time to make a good attempt at it. If the learner continues to struggle the teacher gives a helpful prompt, either from the meaning of the story or sentence or from the form of the word. When the learner finally reads the word correctly the teacher then praises the attempt.

If the learner is reading silently, then a part of the text is read and there is a discussion of what has just been read and prediction of the next part of the text.

### Independent Reading

In **independent reading** the learner chooses a book to read and quietly gets on with reading it. During this quiet period of class time, the teacher may also read or may use the time as an opportunity for individual learners to come up to read to the teacher. In beginners' classes there is a set time each day for independent reading and learners are expected to read out of class as well. Other names for extended independent reading are **sustained silent reading** (SSR) and **drop everything and read** (DEAR).

Learning to read is also helped by learning to write and learning through listening. In writing as in reading, first language teachers emphasise the communication of messages and expect the learners gradually to approximate normal writing over a period of time.

Research indicates that the best age to learn to read is about six to seven years old. Starting early at five has no long-term advantages and may make it more difficult for some learners to experience success in reading. At the age of about six or seven children are intellectually ready to begin reading.

It should be clear from this description that native speakers learning to read have the advantage of bringing a lot of language knowledge and a lot of experience to learning to read. They might have the disadvantage of beginning to learn a complex skill when they may not be quite ready for it.

## Learning to Read in Another Language

There are numerous factors that affect the difficulty of learning to read in another language. Table 1.1 focuses on three factors but as the footnote to the table suggests, there are other factors that are important particularly when working with a group of learners. Let us look at the factors in Table 1.1 by focusing on a learner from a particular language background, Thai, who is in the very early stages of learning English. The learner is 12 years old and can already read fluently in Thai.

A Thai learner beginning to read English will know very little English vocabulary. There are English loan words in Thai like *free*, but a Thai learner probably does not realise that they have an English origin. This means that the initial reading material will need to be much more controlled than the material aimed at young native speakers of English who already know close to five thousand words. A Thai learner may also need much more preparation or pre-teaching before they start on their reading. These are all disadvantages. There are, however, numerous advantages that the Thai learner has. First, the Thai learner can already read Thai and so knows a lot about reading. Thai is an alphabetic language so the Thai learner is already very familiar with the alphabetic principle; that is, that letters can represent sounds and these can go together to make up words. Thai script is not related to English script, so the Thai learner will have to spend time learning letter shapes. An Italian learner of English does not have this problem because Italian uses substantially the same script as English. Second, if the Thai learner is good at reading Thai, the learner will have many reading strategies like guessing from context, scanning, skimming, and careful decoding which could be carried over to the reading of English if the conditions for reading were suitable. There is evidence, for example, that training in increasing reading speed in the first language can transfer to another language if the materials in the other language are at a suitable level (Bismoko and Nation, 1974; Cramer, 1975). Third, reading is largely a valued and enjoyed activity in Thai society so there may also be positive attitudes to reading carried over to English. Fourth, a 12 year old is much more able to learn to read than a five year old. A 12 year old has much more developed cognitive skills and is much more able to learn from direct instruction. Table 1.1 summarises these characteristics.

## Principles for Teaching Reading

The following principles can guide the design and practice of a reading programme. For another list of principles, see Williams (1986).

### Meaning-focused Input

- Practice and training in reading should be done for a range of reading purposes. A reading course should cover these purposes—reading to search for information (including skimming and scanning), reading to learn, reading for fun, reading to integrate information, reading to critique texts, and reading to write. These are looked at throughout the following chapters.
- Learners should be doing reading that is appropriate to their language proficiency level. The course should include reading simplified material at a range of levels, particularly extensive reading of graded readers. Chapter 4 looks at this in detail.
- Reading should be used as a way of developing language proficiency. Learners should read with 98 percent coverage of the vocabulary in the text so that they can learn the remaining 2 percent through guessing from context (Chapter 3).

**Table 1.1** L1/L2 Differences for an Individual Beginning to Read

| Characteristics | General effects | Particular effects |
|---|---|---|
| L1 beginning readers already know a lot of the language they are beginning to read (sounds, vocabulary, grammar, discourse). L2 learners do not. | Learning to read an L2 involves a great deal of language learning. | L2 learners need very controlled texts. L2 learners need a greater amount of pre-reading activities. |
| L2 beginners can already read in their L1. | L2 beginners have general cognitive skills. They have preconceptions and attitudes to reading. They have language specific skills. There will be interference and facilitation effects between the L1 and L2. | L2 beginners do not need to learn what they can transfer from the L1. They may need to change their attitudes to reading. Learners may have to learn a different writing system. |
| L2 beginners are usually older than L1 beginners. | L2 learners have greater metalinguistic and metacognitive awareness. | It is easy to transfer L1 skills. L2 learners can use more explicit approaches and tools like dictionaries. |

This table has been kept simple by focusing on only one learner who is just beginning to read. It is more complicated if you have several learners with different L1s, different L2 proficiencies, different L1 reading proficiencies, and different motivations for reading.

### Meaning-focused Output

- Reading should be related to other language skills. The course should involve listening, speaking and writing activities related to the reading. See, for example, Simcock (1993) using the **ask and answer** technique and several others described later in this book.

### Language-focused Learning

- Learners should be helped to develop the skills and knowledge needed for effective reading. The course should work on the sub-skills of reading and the language features needed to read, including phonemic awareness activities, phonics, spelling practice (Chapter 2), vocabulary learning using word cards, and grammar study. Some of this can be done through intensive reading (Chapter 3).
- Learners should be given training and practice in a range of reading strategies. These strategies could include—previewing, setting a purpose, predicting, posing questions, connecting to background knowledge, paying attention to text structure, guessing words from context,

critiquing, and reflecting on the text. Janzen and Stoller (1998) describe a similar list of strategies.

- Learners should be given training and practice in integrating a range of strategies. Learners should be familiar with a strategy package procedure like reciprocal teaching or concept-oriented reading (CORI) (see Chapter 3).
- Learners should become familiar with a range of text structures, such as those used in newspaper reports, stories, recounts and information reports.

*Fluency Development*

- Learners should be helped and pushed to develop fluency in reading. They need to read material that is very familiar and contains no unknown language features. There should also be speed reading practice in word recognition and in reading for understanding. These can include activities like speed reading, repeated reading, paired reading, scanning, and skimming. Chapter 5 focuses on reading fluency.
- Learners should enjoy reading and feel motivated to read. Learners should have access to interesting texts and be involved in activities like listening to stories, independent reading, and shared reading (blown-up books). Native-speaking children like to read scary books, comics and cartoons, books about sports and magazines about popular culture (Worthy, Moorman and Turner, 1999). These are not usually found at school.
- Learners should read a lot. This can be monitored and encouraged through the use of extensive reading and issue logs.

We will examine these principles in detail in later chapters of this book. A well-thought out reading course can be the core of the language programme as it can give rise to activities in the other skills of listening, speaking, and writing, and can provide the opportunity for a useful, deliberate focus on language features. It can quickly become an effective means of showing that language learning can be successful and enjoyable. The four strands of meaning-focused input, meaning-focused output, language-focused learning, and fluency development are discussed at length in Chapter 1 of the companion volume to this book, *Teaching ESL/EFL Listening and Speaking* (Nation and Newton, 2009).

# CHAPTER 2

# Learning to Recognise and Spell Words

An essential part of the reading skill is the skill of being able to recognise written forms and to connect them with their spoken forms and their meanings. This involves recognising known words and also deciphering unfamiliar words.

There has been considerable debate in first language reading over the role and nature of direct systematic teaching of word recognition skills. See Moorman, Blanton and McLaughlin (1994) for an example of this. There is also debate over the role of language-focused activities, such as reading aloud (see Griffin, 1992; Rounds, 1992). The position taken in this book is that there needs to be a balance of the four strands of meaning-focused input, meaning-focused output, language-focused learning and fluency development, and there is thus a role for appropriate amounts of formal word recognition instruction. The principles that should guide this teaching are that most attention can be given to rules and items that occur frequently, are simple, and are regular.

## Prerequisites for Formal Reading Instruction

To be able to benefit from instruction on spelling rules, learners need to: (1) know at least some of the letter shapes; (2) be aware that words are made up of separable sounds (phonemic awareness); (3) know basic English writing conventions (we read from left to right, beginning at the top and moving down the page); and (4) know the spoken forms of most of the words that will be met in the initial stages of reading.

*Learning Letter Shapes*

If a second language learner is already able to read in their first language, and their first language uses the same alphabet as English, then little if any letter shape learning will be needed. A native speaker of Malay who can read Malay already knows the letter shapes needed for reading English. They may have to apply different spelling-sound rules to these shapes but the written forms are not a problem. Learners who are not literate in their first language, or whose language uses a different writing system, like Arabic or Japanese, may need to learn to recognise the letter shapes. Because of the detailed recognition skills that are needed, it may be most effective to teach learners how to write the letters rather than just rely on reception. Activities can include tracing over letters; repeated copying of letters of the alphabet; delayed copying (Hill, 1969) where the learners look, look away, and write from memory; letter matching of flash cards (find the pairs); and letter dictation. Letters of similar shapes *p, d, b, g,* should not be learned at the same time as they are likely to interfere with each other. There may be some value in practising letter patterns, for example, ⟿⟿⟿⟿, or ℓℓℓℓℓℓ, but this is probably more useful for cursive writing and developing writing fluency.

*Phonemic Awareness*

**Phonemic awareness** is the knowledge that spoken words are made up of sounds that can be separated, that is, that /kæt/ (cat) is made up of the sounds /k æ t/. If the learner can already read in their first language, and the writing system of the first language is alphabetic, the learner will already have phonemic awareness. To get a clearer idea of the nature of phonemic awareness, see Table 2.1 which describes two tests of phonemic awareness.

In essence, phonemic awareness is not awareness of particular sounds. It is awareness of the general principle that words are made up of separable sounds. It is likely that learners who are not literate in their L1 but who are above the age of seven or eight will already have phonemic awareness in their L1 but this should be checked. Learners who are between four and six years old could be tested for phonemic awareness and, if necessary, could be given phonemic awareness activities (see Table 2.2). Phonemic awareness and letter knowledge are the two best predictors of how well first language children just entering school will do at learning to read during the first two years of school. Phonemic awareness training can have positive long-term effects on spelling.

In the vast majority of cases, learners of English as a second language will not need phonemic awareness activities because they will already have this knowledge.

**Table 2.1** Tests of Phonemic Awareness

*Phoneme deletion test* (Bruce, 1964)

What word would remain if this sound was taken away?
(Practice words *c-at, b-r-ight, crie-d*). Takes about 10 minutes.

| | | |
|---|---|---|
| 1. S-t-and (middle) | 11. S-top (first) | 21. Thin-k (last) |
| 2. J-am (first) | 12. Far-m (last) | 22. P-late (first) |
| 3. Fair-y (last) | 13. Mon-k-ey (middle) | 23. S-n-ail (middle) |
| 4. Ha-n-d (middle) | 14. S-pin (first) | 24. B-ring (first) |
| 5. Star-t (last) | 15. For-k (last) | 25. Pin-k (last) |
| 6. Ne-s-t (middle) | 16. C-old (first) | 26. Le-f-t (middle) |
| 7. F-rock (first) | 17. Part-y (last) | 27. Car-d (last) |
| 8. Ten-t (last) | 18. We-n-t (middle) | 28. S-p-oon (middle) |
| 9. Lo-s-t (middle) | 19. F-r-og (middle) | 29. H-ill (first) |
| 10. N-ice (first) | 20. N-ear (first) | 30. Ever-y (last) |

*Phoneme segmentation test* (Yopp, 1988)

Today we're going to play a different word game. I'm going to say a word, and I want you to break the word apart. You are going to tell me each sound in the word in order. For example, if I say *old*, you will say *o-l-d*. Let's try a few words together.

(Three more examples are given *ride, go, man*) Total score = 22. Takes about 5–10 minutes.

| | | | |
|---|---|---|---|
| dog | lay | keep | race |
| fine | zoo | no | three |
| she | job | wave | in |
| grew | ice | that | at |
| red | top | me | by |
| sat | do | | |

**Table 2.2** Phonemic Awareness Activities

**Activities**
The most basic procedures involve: (1) the teacher saying separate sounds (/t/ /e/ /n/) and the learner putting the separate heard sounds together to make a familiar word (ten) (i.e. phoneme blending); and (2) the learner saying the separate sounds of a word for the teacher to guess what the word is (i.e. phoneme segmentation). These activities can be done as a game. Other activities include:

1 phoneme isolation (What is the first sound in *run*?)
2 phoneme identification (What sound is the same in *rat, run, ripe*?)
3 phoneme deletion (What word do we have if we take /t/ out of *stand*?)

**Principles**
• Phonemic awareness activities should be done with known words.
• Phonemic awareness activities should be fun.

*Writing Conventions*

English has the following writing conventions. Not all languages follow the same conventions.

1. Writing goes from left to right (cf. Arabic—right to left, Japanese—top to bottom).
2. The lines of writing come one under the other starting from the top of the page (cf. Japanese).
3. The pages go from front to back (cf. Japanese—back to front).
4. Words are separated by spaces (cf. Thai—no spaces between words).
5. Sentences begin with a capital letter and end with a full stop, question mark, or exclamation mark.
6. Quotation marks are used to signal speech or citation.
7. English has upper case (capital) letters and lower case (small) letters. The use of capital letters may carry an extra meaning.
8. Sentences are organised into paragraphs.
9. In formal and academic writing there are conventions that need to be learned, such as the use of bold and italics, the use of headings and sub-headings, the use of indentation, the use of footnotes, the use of references, and page numbering.

In early reading, learners may need to be checked for knowledge of these conventions, and some may need to be pointed out and explained.

*Spoken Language and Reading*

The experience approach to reading is based on the idea that when learning to read, learners should bring a lot of experience and knowledge to their reading so that they only have to focus on small amounts of new information. Sylvia Ashton-Warner's (1963) approach to teaching young native speakers to read is an excellent example of this. Here are the steps in her approach.

1. Each learner draws a picture illustrating something that recently happened to them or something that they are very interested in.
2. One by one the learners take their picture to the teacher who asks them what it is about.
3. The teacher then writes the learner's description below the picture exactly as the learner said it using the same words the learner said, even if it is non-standard English.
4. This then becomes the learner's reading text for that day. The learner reads it back to the teacher and then takes it away to practise reading it, and to read it to classmates, friends and family.

5. These pictures and texts all written by the same learner are gathered together to be a personal reading book for that learner.

Note that most of the knowledge needed to read and comprehend the text is directly within the experience of the learner. The ideas come from the learner, the words and sentences come from the learner, and the organisation of the text comes from the learner. The only learning needed is to match the new written forms provided by the teacher with this knowledge.

It is possible to learn to read a foreign language without being able to speak it, but learning to read is much easier if the learner already has spoken control of the language features that are being met in the reading. Reading texts used with young native speakers of English use language that is already known to them and are on topics that interest them. However, young native speakers learning to read have an oral vocabulary size of around 5,000 words. Non-native speakers will have a very much smaller English vocabulary and so if native-speaker texts are used to teach second language reading, they need to be checked to see if they contain known and useful vocabulary.

## Phonics and the Alphabetic Principle

Learning phonics is learning the systematic relationships between written letters and sounds, for example, learning that the written form p is usually pronounced /p/. At a very general level, learning phonics means learning the alphabetic principle, that is that letters and groups of letters represent sounds in a largely systematic way. At a detailed level, learning phonics involves learning the range of spelling-sound correspondences that exist in a particular language.

Some languages like Chinese do not follow the alphabetic principle. They do not have separate letters that represent the individual sounds that go together to make a spoken word. Other languages follow the alphabetic principle in a very regular way. The Maori language, for example, has 12 consonant sounds and five vowel sounds (10 if long and short versions of vowels are not counted as the same sound). These are represented by 11 consonant letters and five vowel letters. The only exceptions to a one letter-one sound (not necessarily one phoneme) rule are that the letters wh represent a sound which is not /w/ plus /h/, and the letters ng represent a sound /ŋ/ which is not /n/ plus /g/. After a few lessons in Maori pronunciation, it is possible for anyone familiar with the English alphabet to learn all the Maori spelling-sound correspondences in a few minutes.

This is an over-simplification because there are different dialects of Maori. However, there are frequent, systematic relationships in English that can provide a good basis for effective phonics instruction. Here are some English spelling-sound rules that are regular and very, very frequent. The letter b̲ is pronounced /b/, f̲—/f/, k̲—/k/, m̲—/m/, v̲—/v/.

There are exceptions to these rules, but most of the exceptions are rule-based (bb̲—/b/, mm̲—/m/) or do not occur in many words.

As a fluent reader of English you already know the regular rules and can thus make a reasonable pronunciation of written words that you have probably never seen before—*lyncean, glogg, cordwain, sclerotium, tussah.*

If a teacher wants to do some phonics instruction, it is important to know what the most useful rules in English are and to be able to determine whether it is better to deal with a particular word phonically or simply to encourage learners to memorise the spelling of the whole word. Appendix 1 lists the important rules for English and provides some guidance and practice in applying the rules. By working through Appendix 1 you should be able to do the following things.

1. Make an ordered systematic syllabus for phonics instruction. In particular, decide what phonics rules deserve attention early in a reading programme.
2. Be aware of the most common exceptions to the rules.
3. Where there are conflicting rules, for example a̲—/aː/, a̲—/æ/, decide which one should get attention first.
4. Decide whether a word is regularly spelled or not. In other words, work out the learning burden of its written form.
5. Interpret errors in learners' reading aloud to see if they are rule-based or not.

## The Role of Phonics in a Reading Programme

Phonics can fit into a reading programme in the following ways.

*Isolated Words and Words in Texts*

- Help learners in using phonics to read specially chosen isolated words.
- Introduce phonics with known words.
- Ask students to read interesting texts that use regular spelling-sound correspondences such as Dr Seuss books.

*Individual and Class*

- Use phonics in one-to-one reading instruction as a part of reading a text.
- Carry out class teaching of the most frequent, simple, regular spelling-sound correspondences.

*Word Attack Skills*

- Teach learners to sound out all the sounds in a word.
- Teach learners to concentrate on the first letters of a word.
- Where possible, use phonics when giving help with difficult words.

*Outlandish Proposals*

- Use regularised English as an intermediary step.
- Allow invented spellings that follow rules—the rule is more important than the items.

Word recognition when reading is helped by familiarity with what is being read (from having read it before or from listening to it being read), by context clues coming from the meaning of what is being read, by being able to recognise some words as complete units, and by being able to decode words phonically. It is worth drawing on all these sources of help because ultimately it is the quantity of successful reading that will contribute most to the development of reading skills, and using all these sources is more likely to guarantee success.

As phonics involves spelling-sound relationships, it is significant both for learning to read and for learning to spell.

## Spelling: Productive Phonics

Being familiar with spelling-sound correspondences can be seen as a receptive skill in that it relates to the receptive skill of reading. The productive equivalent of this part of the reading skill is spelling, which is part of the skill of writing.

There has been considerable research with native speakers on the learning of spelling and the definitive collection of research reviews is Brown and Ellis's (1994) *Handbook of Spelling*. From an applied linguistics perspective, the study of research on spelling is rewarding not only for the information it provides on the teaching and learning of spelling, but also because it provides valuable insights into many of the central issues involved in second language learning. Spelling is a very limited and clearly defined area, involving only 26 letters and a definable set of combinations of letters. Working within this limited area makes the issues clearer and easier to deal with in a comprehensive way.

Table 2.3 lists the most important of these with a brief summary of findings from L1 research. Let us look briefly at some of these.

*Deliberate and Incidental Learning*

In the learning of both grammatical and vocabulary items there has been debate over the roles of incidental learning (acquisition in Krashen's

**Table 2.3** Issues in Spelling that Apply to Other Language Levels

| Issues | Findings |
| --- | --- |
| Deliberate versus incidental learning | Deliberate analytic learning can speed up learning and can help with learning problems. Regular tests help. Most learning is incidental. Substantial reading improves spelling. |
| System learning versus item learning | Some words can be dealt with by rules, others have to be learned as unique items. The unpredictability of the English spelling system is a major obstacle to learning to spell. |
| A single kind of learning versus interactive systems | Alphabetic learning interacts with lexical learning. |
| The effect of other levels of language on this level and this level on others | Phonological awareness affects spelling and has long-term effects on spelling. Spelling affects word recognition. Poor spellers have problems in writing—they use avoidance strategies. Phonological awareness affects reading and reading can affect phonological awareness. Writing the letter shapes helps learning. |
| The direction of the effect | Spelling affects use, use affects spelling. |
| The effect of the origin of the feature | Etymology affects spelling. |
| The treatment of irregularity | Some high frequency items are irregular. Irregular items are learned as lexical units. |
| The effect of frequency on the type of storage | Highly frequent items, even regular ones, are stored as lexical items. Regular low frequency items are dealt with by rules. |
| The effect of age on learning | Older learners are better at deliberate learning. |
| The role of developmental sequences | Complex items need to be learned through a series of stages. |
| The treatment of error | Letting students invent spellings can have positive effects. |
| The effect of the first language | The writing system of the first language can have positive and negative effects on learning the second language. |

(1981) terms) and deliberate learning. Some argue that incidental learning is what really matters and that at best deliberate learning can only play an indirect secondary role. In vocabulary learning, however, there is considerable evidence supporting the deliberate learning of vocabulary as part of a well-balanced programme (Elgort, 2007). First language research on the learning of spelling also supports having both deliberate and incidental learning. Although most learning of the many sound-spelling correspondences is picked up incidentally and good readers are usually good spellers, deliberate analytic learning can speed up learning and can help with learning difficulties.

*System Learning and Item Learning*

Partly as a result of the impact of corpus linguistics, there has been considerable debate over whether learners develop substantial control of a complex grammatical system or whether what seems to be grammar learning is really the accumulation of knowledge of numerous collocations. That is, much language use is not rule-based but is based on the use of pre-fabricated units (see Pinker, 1999, for an interesting discussion of this). Research on the learning of complex words like *decompose, combinability* and *unrefugeelike* suggests that high frequency complex words are stored as whole, ready-made units. Low frequency complex words are recreated each time they are met or used. That is, low frequency items are dealt with according to systematic rules, while high frequency items are dealt with by accessing memorised complete units. Frequency and complexity combine nicely in this argument. High frequency items are relatively small in number so there are not too many to store. If they were processed according to rules, because they are very frequent a lot of processing time would be spent dealing with them and that would be difficult. Thus storing them as ready-made items is the most efficient option. Low frequency items are very numerous. There are too many of them to store as ready-made complex units. However, low frequency items make up only a small proportion of the running words so dealing with them according to rules does not occupy too much on-line processing time. Thus, processing them according to rules is the best option.

Research on spelling supports this high frequency/low frequency distinction. Many high frequency words are irregularly spelled and must be stored as memorised items. Low frequency words tend to be more regularly spelled and can be dealt with by the application of rules.

*First Language Effects on Second Language Learning*

In its simplest form, the contrastive analysis hypothesis argued that second language learning can be strongly affected by first language knowledge.

Where there are similarities between languages, second language learning will be easier. Where there are differences, second language learning will be more difficult. Complications in the hypothesis arise from the ways in which a second language is learned, and in the nature of the similarities and differences between the two languages.

There is evidence of positive and negative effects of the first language on the second at the levels of pronunciation, vocabulary, grammar, and discourse. Spelling is no exception, and there is plenty of evidence of first language spellings having both positive and negative effects according to the degrees of similarity and difference between the language items and rules.

## Learning to Spell

English spelling is difficult. Although there are many rules, there are also many irregularities and decision points where competing rules need to be chosen. Learning how to spell in more regularly spelled languages like Indonesian, Samoan or Finnish is a much easier task. If learners have poor spelling skills, they will typically avoid writing tasks, and when writing will avoid words that they find difficult to spell.

One way of organising an approach to spelling improvement is to ensure that spelling is dealt with across the four strands of meaning-focused input, meaning-focused output, language-focused learning and fluency development.

## Spelling and Meaning-focused Input

The more learners read, the more their spelling will improve. Continual receptive exposure to the written forms of words provides a useful basis for later written production (Cunningham and Stanovich, 1991). In the early stages of learning to read English as an L1, the number of words learners can read is much greater than the number they can spell and the size of this gap persists for several years.

## Spelling and Meaning-focused Output

Spelling is particularly important for writing and at the very least, having to write can make learners aware of gaps in their spelling knowledge.

In the early stages of writing by young native speakers, teachers accept the invented spellings they produce as useful steps on the way to more accurate spelling.

Writing activities that can help with spelling are copying, delayed copying, read and write from memory, dictation, the various forms of guided writing, writing with the help of a dictionary, and free writing. Too much attention to spelling when responding to learners' writing can result in an unwillingness to write or avoidance strategies where learners only use very familiar words.

## Spelling and Language-focused Learning

There are numerous techniques for giving deliberate attention to spelling. The critical factor is making sure that there is an appropriate balance of each of the four strands so that there is some deliberate attention to spelling but this attention does not become excessive. Deliberate attention to spelling can include the following.

*The Deliberate Memorisation of the Spelling of Individual Words*

Cover and Retrieve

The learner writes a list of difficult to spell words down the left-hand side of the page. The first letter or two of each word is written next to it, for example

```
yacht        y
occurrence   o
```

The words are studied and then covered and each word is written from memory using the first letter clue. The first letter is written again so that the activity can be repeated.

```
yacht        yacht   y
```

Using Analogies

Working with the teacher or in pairs or small groups, the learners think of known words that share similar spelling features to words that they have difficulty in spelling. For example, if learning to spell *apply*, the learners think of the known words *reply*, *supply*, etc.

Using Word Parts

For advanced learners, drawing attention to word-building units can help. For example, *separate* contains the root *par* which is also in *part*. The spelling is therefore *separate* not *seperate*.

Pronouncing the Word in the Way it is Spelled

A word like *yacht* can be deliberately mispronounced as /yæt čt/ as a kind of mnemonic for the spelling.

Visualising

Learners look at a word, close their eyes and try to see the spelling of the word in their mind. If a part of the word is particularly difficult to remember, try to think of that part in a striking colour such as red.

### Tests

Teachers can have regular tests to encourage learners to work on spelling. These can be dictation tests or individualised tests as in the cover and retrieve technique where the learners each give the teacher a list of words on one sheet and on another sheet a list of the first letters of the words. The sheet with the first letters is used for the test, and the other for marking.

### *The Deliberate Study of Regular Correspondences and Rules*

### Noticing Patterns

Words following a similar set of sound-spelling correspondences are grouped together so that learners see several examples of the same correspondence, for example

day, play, say, may, stay

Learners' involvement in such noticing can be deepened by getting learners to work in pairs grouping such words from a mixed list, by dictating the words to the learners, by getting learners to suggest other words that follow the pattern, and by following up these activities with a dictation test drawing on a variety of patterns.

### Studying Rules

A few very common complicated rules deserve a bit of deliberate study, particularly for advanced learners. The most useful of these rules are:

1. *i* before *e* except after *c*
2. free and checked vowels.

The rule for free and checked vowels is rather complicated but it is very useful because it provides explanations for the doubling of consonants when adding affixes, the function of final silent *e*, and the spelling and pronunciation of a large number of words. To understand the rule it is necessary to know what the free vowels are and what the checked (or limited or short) vowels are. The free vowels *a e i o u* are pronounced / ei i: ai ou u:/, which is the same as their names (for example, the name for the letter *a* is pronounced /ei/). The checked vowels *a e i o u* are pronounced /æ e i o u/. Some people call free and checked vowels long and short vowels but this is misleading from a phonological point of view because there is much more than a length difference between the two sets of pronunciations.

Here are the rules associated with the free and checked vowels. These rules apply only to stressed syllables.

1. Free vowels occur in the pattern

   free vowel+consonant+vowel.
   *date, medium*

2. Checked vowels occur in the patterns

   checked vowel+consonant with nothing following the consonant
   *hat, fetch, sip, lot, shut*

   checked vowel+consonant+consonant (+consonant)+vowel

   *happen, better,*
   *sitting, bottle, funny*

Note (a) the single letter *x* behaves like two consonants, (b) *y* in final position acts as a vowel.

If you have understood the above explanation, you should be able to answer these questions. (Answers are supplied on page 24.)

1. What job does final silent *e* do in the following words? *plate, scene, fine, home, tune*
2. Why do you have to double the final consonant in the stem when you add *y* to the following words? *fun, fat, slop, bag*
3. Why don't you have to double the final consonant when you add *ing* or *ed* to the following words? Look at each word carefully. *weed, lengthen, push, hope*
4. Why is *occurrence* correct and not *occurence*?
5. Why is *exclamation* correct and not *exclammation*?

There are exceptions to the rules and it may be that the best use of the free/checked rule is as a way of explaining and helping to learn difficult words that follow the rules. The free and checked rules are items AV3, AV14, AV18, AV24, AV1, AV8, AV13, AV16, AV23 in Appendix 1. The exceptions are BV7.

*Strategy Training*

Learners should have familiar and well-practised strategies to follow to: (1) commit the spelling of a newly met word to memory; (2) find the spelling of a needed word when writing; and (3) decide how to pronounce a newly met word when reading. These strategies should be made up of activities that have already been practised in class.

A Strategy for Memorising Spellings

The activities described above in the section on deliberate memorisation can be put into a sequence that can be followed as far as is necessary for each word. That is, first, the learner should close their eyes and try to visualise the word, that is, make a retrieval. Second, the learner should think of similarly spelled words. Third, if possible, the word can be broken into parts to see if knowing the parts helps remember the spelling. Fourth, if the word is really difficult to remember, it can be added to a list to use with the cover and retrieve technique. Alternatively, it can be placed on a word card for spaced recall practice. Ideally, learners should get plenty of practice using this strategy, and reflecting on it by thinking about it and talking about its application with other learners.

A Strategy for Finding the Spelling of a Word

Before looking up the spelling of a word in a dictionary, the learner should make an informed guess about how the word might be spelled. This can be done by thinking about other known words that sound the same and, if possible, checking that the spelling fits known rules.

A Strategy for Deciding how to Pronounce a Written Form

First, if the word looks like known words, the learner can try that pronunciation. Second, breaking the word into parts could help with getting the stress in the right place. Third, seek confirmation by asking someone who might know or by using a dictionary.

*Spelling and Fluency Development*

Fluency in spelling will come from large quantities of reading and writing, and from fluency practice in reading and writing. A typical writing fluency development activity is **ten minute writing** where learners write as much as they can on an easy topic in a regular, timed ten-minute period. The teacher does not correct spelling errors or grammatical errors, but responds to the content of the text encouraging the learner to write more. The speed of writing in words per minute is kept on a personal graph by each learner and their goal is to see their speed in words per minute increase. This is done about three times a week.

## Designing a Focused Spelling Programme

If spelling is a significant problem for learners, it may be worthwhile giving it some focused, planned special attention. Numerous studies looking at spelling and on other learning issues have shown the positive effects of a balanced, focused programme. Table 2.4 lists general principles that can be applied to any focused programme. These are organised under the headings *affective, cognitive* and *social* to make them easier to remember and to put into practice the idea that an effective programme will approach a problem from several perspectives; in this case, the attitudes and feelings of the learners, the knowledge involved, and the support that others can give. Table 2.4 also gives examples of application of the principles. There could be a third column in Table 2.4 and that would show the particular applications to a spelling programme. Let us take an example. Under the applications of the affective principle, *Keep learners motivated*, there is the application, *Do mastery testing*. Mastery testing involves repeated learning and testing until learners gain near perfect scores in what they have to learn. For mastery testing to work, there needs to be a clearly defined set of things to learn and there needs to be repeated and varied opportunities to do this learning. Mastery testing could be applied to a spelling programme in the following way. For a particular course, the focus may be the regularly spelled words in the first one thousand words of English. Those words would be ones that could be completely described by sections A and B of Appendix 1. Each week a few correspondences would be focused on and these would be tested by word dictation tests to see if learners had mastered the rules. If they did not score 90 percent or more on a 20-item test, they could sit another test focusing on the same correspondences. Before sitting another test, the teacher or learners could analyse the errors in the previous test and the learners could work on some practice items.

Table 2.4 can also be used as a basis for evaluating a focused programme. Not all of the applications need be used but there should be variety and balance.

**Table 2.4** Features of a Good Intensive Learning Programme

| Principles | Applications |
| --- | --- |
| **Affective** | |
| Keep learners motivated | Praise success |
| | Give quick feedback |
| | Do mastery testing |
| | Measure progress |
| | Record success on graphs or tables |
| Make learning fun | Use attractive aids |
| | Have amusing competitions |
| **Cognitive** | |
| Encourage thoughtful processing | Use rich associations, mnemonics, rules, retrieval, visualisation, deliberate learning, movement |
| | Use both analytic and holistic techniques |
| | Isolate and focus on problems |
| Plan for repetition and revision | Give regular practice |
| | Plan increasingly spaced revision |
| Provide training | Combine activities into strategies |
| | Train learners in strategy use |
| | Get learners to reflect on learning |

*(Continued overleaf)*

**Table 2.4** Continued.

| Principles | Applications |
|---|---|
| Organise the items to learn in helpful ways | Group the items to learn into manageable blocks<br>Avoid interference<br>Group helpfully related items together |
| Plan for transfer of training | Provide fluency training |
| **Social** | |
| Provide peer support | Do peer tutoring<br>Get learners to report progress to others<br>Organise support groups |
| Aim for individual responsibility | Let learners choose what and how to learn<br>Encourage autonomy |

Note that the multi-focused approach in Table 2.4 can be applied to other things besides spelling, for example, learning to read, pronunciation, writing and so on. Spelling is only a small part of learning a language and for some learners it may not be an important focus, either because they have no problem with it or because writing is not a major part of their language use. What should be clear from this chapter is that spelling is no different from other aspects of language use. If it is given attention, this attention should be balanced and in proportion to other focuses.

---

**Answers to the Questions on Spelling on page 21**
1. Keeps the preceding vowel as a free vowel.
2. Because *y* acts as a vowel and the preceding consonant needs to be doubled so the preceding vowel remains as a checked vowel.
3. In *weed* and *hope* the vowels are free vowels so they do not need doubling of the following consonant to keep them checked. In *push, sh* acts as two consonants and keeps *u* checked. In *lengthen* the stressed syllable is the first syllable of the word and so adding -*ing* to the second syllable does not have an effect because the rule applies only to stressed syllables.
4. The *u* in *occurrence* is a checked vowel. It needs to be followed by two consonants (double *r*) so that the following vowel *e* does not make it a free vowel. If there was no double *r* the pronunciation would change.
5. It is the second *a* in *exclamation* that is in the stressed syllable and the free/checked rule only applies to stressed syllables.

# CHAPTER 3

# Intensive Reading

Intensive study of reading texts can be a means of increasing learners' knowledge of language features and their control of reading strategies. It can also improve their comprehension skill. It fits into the language-focused learning strand of a course. The classic procedure for **intensive reading** is the grammar-translation approach where the teacher works with the learners, using the first language to explain the meaning of a text, sentence by sentence. Used on suitable texts and following useful principles, this can be a very useful procedure as long as it is only a part of the reading programme and is complemented by other language-focused learning and by extensive reading for language development and extensive reading for fluency development.

At its worst, intensive reading focuses on comprehension of a particular text with no thought being given to whether the features studied in this text will be useful when reading other texts. Such intensive reading usually involves translation and thus comprehension of the text. So, one goal of intensive reading may be comprehension of the text. The use of translation makes sure that learners understand, and when the learners do some of the translation themselves, it allows the teacher to check whether they understand.

Intensive reading may also have another goal and that is to determine what language features will get attention in the course. That is, the language features that are focused on in each text become the language syllabus for the course. This has several positive aspects. First, the language features are set in the communicative context of a text. The text can be used to show how the language features contribute to the communicative purpose of the text and this can be good preparation for subsequent writing activities. Second, choosing features in this way is likely to avoid the interference between vocabulary items or grammatical features that can occur when topic-centred syllabus design is used.

There are also negative aspects to letting texts determine the language features of a course. First, the features given attention to may be an uncontrolled mixture of useful and not very useful items. That is, high frequency and low frequency vocabulary, frequent grammatical items and very infrequent or irregular grammatical items may get equal attention. Second, the topic of the text determines the salience of the items and the teaching gets directed towards this text rather than what will be useful in a range of texts.

If intensive reading is to be done well, the major principle determining the focus of the teaching should be that the focus is on items that will occur in a wide range of texts. The teacher should ask "How does today's teaching make *tomorrow's* text easier?". There are four ways of putting this important principle into practice.

1. Focus on items that occur with high frequency in the language as a whole (see Table 3.1 for examples). Such items will occur often in many different texts.
2. Focus on strategies that can be used with most texts (see Table 3.1 for examples).

**Table 3.1** Useful Focuses in Extensive Reading

| Focus | Items | Strategies |
| --- | --- | --- |
| Comprehension | Question types<br>Question forms | Predicting<br>Standardised reading procedures |
| Sound-spelling | Regular sound-spelling correspondences | Spelling rules<br>Free/checked vowels |
| Vocabulary | High frequency vocabulary<br>Underlying meanings of words | Guessing<br>Noting and learning on cards<br>Word parts<br>Dictionary use |
| Grammar and cohesion | High frequency grammatical features | Dealing with sources of difficulty (clause insertion, what does what?, coordination, cohesion) |
| Information content | Topic type constituents | Topic type |
| Genre | Features that typify this type of text | Generalise to writing |

3. Quickly deal with or ignore infrequent items.
4. Make sure that the same items and strategies get attention in several different texts.

## Focuses in Intensive Reading

Intensive work on a reading text can focus on the following aspects. These will be looked at in more detail in the rest of this chapter and in other chapters in this book.

1. *Comprehension.* Intensive reading can aim at understanding a particular text.
2. *Regular and irregular sound-spelling relations.* This can be done through the teaching of phonics, through teaching spelling rules, and through reading aloud. This is covered in Chapter 2 on sounds and spelling.
3. *Vocabulary.* Learners' attention can be drawn to useful words, and the underlying meaning and use of these words can be explained. Words from the text could be assigned for later study.
4. *Grammar.* Difficult grammatical features can be explained and analysed.
5. *Cohesion.* Learners can practise interpreting what pronouns refer to in the text, what the conjunction relationships between sentences are, and how different words are used to refer to the same idea.
6. *Information structure.* Certain texts contain certain kinds of information. Newspaper reports, for example, can describe what happened, what led to the happening, what the likely effects will be, who was involved, and when and where it happened. Learners can be helped to identify these different kinds of information. This is covered in Chapter 9 on topic types.
7. *Genre features.* The vocabulary, grammatical features, cohesive features and information all contribute to the communicative effect of a text. Intensive reading can focus on how the text achieves its communicative purpose through these features and what this communicative purpose is.
8. *Strategies.* Intensive reading can be used to help learners develop useful reading strategies. By working intensively on a text, learners can practise the steps in guessing from context, using a dictionary, simplifying difficult sentences and taking notes. They can also receive training in integrated packages of strategies. In this chapter, strategies are included in the sections on comprehension, vocabulary, grammar and cohesion.

The discussion and explanation of the text need not be done using the first language, but use of the first language makes explanation much easier. The effect of this teaching should be to get learners to actually learn specific features or to make them aware of these so that they notice them in future reading and thus have a greater chance of learning them later.

Language-focused learning for reading can occur through intensive reading with a teacher and it can also occur through written exercises accompanying a text.

## Features of a Good Intensive Reading Exercise

Let us look at what a good reading exercise should do.

1. A good reading exercise directs the learners' attention to features of the text that can be found in almost any text, or to strategies for dealing with any text, with the aim "to develop in the language learner the ability to comprehend *texts*, not to guide him to comprehension of *a text*" (Davies and Widdowson, 1974: 172). To put it another way, when learners study a reading text, we want them to gain knowledge that will help them to understand tomorrow's reading text. We want them to learn things that apply to all texts. We want them to gain knowledge of the language and ways of dealing with the language rather than an understanding of a particular message. If a reading exercise does not focus on generalisable features of a text, it does not provide much opportunity for any useful, cumulative learning to take place. This requirement is particularly important for teaching reading.

2. A good reading exercise directs the learners' attention to the reading text. That is, the learners need to read the text or at least part of it in order to do the exercise. It is also important that some reading exercises require the learners to consider parts of the text in relation to their wider context, that is, other parts of the text, and information from outside the text.

3. A good reading exercise provides the teacher and the learners with useful information about the learners' performance on the exercise. If the learners were not successful on some parts of the exercise, then they should be aware of what they have to learn in order to do the exercise successfully with another text. Also, the teacher can get guidance from the learners' performance to improve teaching. Good exercises provide useful feedback for the teacher and the learners. Also, if the teacher understands what an exercise is trying to teach, they can judge the value of the exercise according to what they think is important for teaching reading.

4. A good reading exercise is easy to make. Teachers have to choose texts suited to the particular needs of their learners, and if these texts do not have satisfactory exercises, the teachers must make their own. Often teachers may want the learners to work with a textbook that is used in another discipline they are studying, and so they will have to make their own exercises. This should require a minimum of skill and time. If the preparation of language teaching materials becomes the job only of experts, then language teachers will have lost the flexibility needed for successful teaching.

So, a good reading exercise focuses on items or strategies that apply to any text, requires the learners to read the text, provides useful feedback for the learners and the teacher, and is easy to make.

### Are Comprehension Questions Good Reading Exercises?

Comprehension questions in one form or other are one of the language teaching techniques most frequently used to train learners in reading. They can take many forms, namely pronominal questions, yes/no questions, true/false statements, multiple-choice items and blank-filling or completion exercises. However, although comprehension questions may have a role to play in *practising* reading, the various forms of reading comprehension questions are not so effective for *teaching* learners to read. In order to show this, let us look at comprehension questions according to the four features of a good reading exercise. After that, a variety of other reading exercises are described which may also be used in intensive reading.

The basic weakness of comprehension questions is that a simple question form can do so many things. A question can check vocabulary, sentence structure, inference, supposition, the ability to understand the question itself, and many other things. It is not always easy to decide which of these is being asked for in a particular question. Let us now evaluate comprehension questions as a type of exercise by seeing how they fit the four criteria given in the previous section.

1. Comprehension questions are local rather than general. They focus attention on the message of a particular text and, although they may require the learners to use more generalisable knowledge (like the interpretation of reference words or modal verbs), this requirement is usually hidden to the learner, and often to the teacher, by the message-focusing effect of the question. The teacher's aim should be to help the learners develop knowledge of the language and its conventions of use, and strategies, so that they can successfully deal with any text that they may meet. This knowledge of the language,

however, is more difficult to gain if the learners' attention is directed not towards the language but towards the meaning or message of a particular text. The motivation to give attention to language features is different from the motivation to give attention to particular messages (George, 1972: 11). Comprehension questions say to the learners "Do you understand this passage?" whereas a good intensive reading exercise should say "Can you handle these language features which are in this passage and other passages?".

2. Generally, comprehension questions direct learners' attention to the reading text, although occasionally some questions are answerable from the learners' own experience without having to refer to the text. Comprehension questions in standardised tests are usually pre-tested to make sure that they cannot be answered without reading the text. Comprehension questions can be designed to make the learners consider more than one sentence in the text in order to find the answer.

3. As comprehension questions can do so many jobs, it is not always clear which job they are doing and thus it is difficult to get useful feedback. Munby (1968) tried to solve this problem by using very carefully constructed multiple-choice comprehension questions.

> By setting carefully constructed distractors we can train [the learners] to reason their way through the linguistic and intellectual problems posed by the text. (p. xxii)

> . . . in comprehension training we want [the learner] to recognize the areas of comprehension error (through the distractors) so that he learns to respond accurately and more maturely to what he reads. (p. xiii)

One of the most important steps in Munby's technique is discussion between the teacher and learners in order to eliminate the distractors.

The value of Munby's technique is that through the discussion it becomes clear to the learners that they have made errors in comprehension and that these errors, *as long as their causes are clearly identified*, can be avoided by mastering recurrent language features. There are three important weaknesses in the technique. First, such comprehension questions are difficult to make. Second, such questions are clearly inefficient in terms of opportunity for *learning* the significance of a particular language feature. For example, there will probably be only one or two questions at the most for one text which focus attention on conjunction relationships, and so the learners will have few opportunities to master them. Third, from the learners' point of view, the most important information that they will gain from making an error is that they made the wrong choice and their interest will be in discovering what the right answer is rather than in discovering what they should do to avoid a similar error in the future. Thus comprehension questions which could give valuable feedback to the learners will be unlikely to do so, because there will always be the more immediate attraction of getting the right answer for that particular item.

4. It is difficult to make good comprehension questions. It takes considerable skill, time, and effort. Thus most teachers who wish to use such exercises will be forced to rely on often unsuitable published material.

In spite of these disadvantages, comprehension questions are useful ways of *practising* reading and of motivating learners to read.

In the rest of this chapter, where possible, examples will be based on the text in Figure 3.1. The text is taken from Chapter 5 of this book.

| | Reading speed |
|---|---|
| 1 | When people read, three types of action are involved—fixations on particular words, jumps (saccades) to the next item to focus on, and regressions (movements back to an item already looked at). A skilled reader reading at around 250–300 words per minute |
| 5 | makes around 95 fixations per 100 words. Most words are fixated on, but function words much less often than content words. The longer the word, the more likely it is to receive a fixation. If the word is really long, it may receive 2 or even 3 fixations. |
| 10 | spends around 200 milliseconds on each fixation (about 5 per second). These vary a lot depending on how difficult a word or sentence is to read. |
| 15 | makes saccadic jumps of around 1.2 words in English (About eight letters. In Finnish, where words are longer, the average jump is 10 letters). This is around the maximum number of letters that can be seen clearly in one fixation. During the jump no items can be focused on. A jump takes about 20 milliseconds. The basic unit in the jump is the word and languages with quite different writing systems (for example, English and Chinese) all tend to have an average of one jump for every 1.2 words. |
| 20 | makes around 15 regressions in every 100 fixations. Regressions occur because the reader made too big a jump (many regressions are only a few letters long), and because there were problems in understanding the text. |
| | There is thus a physiological limit on reading speed where reading involves fixating on most of the words in the text. This is around 330 words per minute. |

**Figure 3.1** Sample Text for Illustrating the Exercises in Chapter 3

## Comprehension of the Text

Typically comprehension questions are used as the major means of focusing on comprehension of the text. The learners read a text and then answer questions about the content of the text. There is a variety of question types that can be used.

*Question Forms*

1. **Pronominal questions** are questions beginning with *who, what, when, how, why*, etc.

   What is a saccade? How long does a fixation take?

   These questions often test writing ability as well as reading ability because the learners must write the answers. The questions can ask for one-word answers, or ask the learners to copy the answers directly from the passage. This makes them easier to mark. The learners can also answer questions using their first language. Instead of questions, commands may be used.

   Explain the three kinds of eye actions.
   Describe a fixation.

2. **Yes/no questions** and alternative questions only need short answers so the learners do not need to have a high level of writing skill.

   Does a fixation take a longer time than a jump?
   Do some words get more than one fixation?
   Does every word get a fixation?

3. **True/false sentences** are similar to yes/no questions. As with yes/no questions the learners have a 50 percent chance of guessing correctly. The learners look at each sentence and decide if it is true or false according to the passage. The learners answer by writing *True* or *False*, or by copying the sentences that are true and not copying the false sentences. This last way provides an opportunity for more learning to take place.

   A good reader makes about ten fixations per second.
   Most jumps are from one word to another.

   The learners may also be asked to rewrite the false sentences making changes so that they are now true.

4. **Multiple-choice sentences** are easy to mark. If four choices are given, the learners have only a 25 percent chance of guessing correctly. If the questions are not well made, often the learners' chances are

higher. Good multiple-choice questions are not easy to make and often they are more difficult than they should be. This is because the wrong choices must seem possible and not stupid. If they are possible then they might be partly correct.

   1. A fixation
      (a) takes about two-tenths of a second
      (b) is about one word long
      (c) is the opposite of a regression
      (d) is longer in Finnish than in English

5. **Sentence completion**. The learners complete sentences by filling the empty spaces to show that they understand the reading passage. The sentences come after the reading passage. There are four different types of sentence completion.

   (i)    The sentences are exact copies of sentences in the passage.
   (ii)   The missing words can be found in the passage.
   (iii)  The sentences are not exactly the same as the sentences in the passage although they talk about the same idea.
   (iv)  The missing words are not in the passage so the learners must use their knowledge of vocabulary to fill the empty spaces.

     A skilled reader makes about ____ fixations per 100 words.
     A skilled reader makes around ____ fixations per minute.

The learners are helped if there is a short line for each letter of the missing word, if the first letter is given and so on.

6. **Information transfer**. The learners complete an information transfer diagram based on the information in the text (Palmer, 1982). Chapter 9 provides examples of information transfer diagrams.
7. **Translation**. The learners must translate the passage into another language. Although translation is often a special skill, it can also show areas of difficulty that the learners have in reading. It also shows clearly where the learners do not have any difficulty. It is a very searching test of understanding, but it includes other skills besides reading.
8. **Précis**. After the learners read the passage they write a short composition about one-quarter of the length of the passage containing all the main ideas that are in the passage. This is called a précis. It can be done as group work. The learners are divided into small groups. Each group makes a list of the main ideas in the passage. Then the class as a whole discusses the main points and the teacher writes them on the blackboard. Then each group writes the précis (Forrester, 1968).

Usually, a summary is made by choosing the main ideas from a text. Chambers and Brigham (1989), however, suggest a more teachable strategy, **summary by deletion**. This involves systematically deleting unimportant parts of the text and using what is left as the text for the summary. The steps are: (1) read the passage and delete all the sentences that merely elaborate the main sentences; (2) delete all unnecessary clauses and phrases from the main sentences; (3) delete all unnecessary words from what remains; (4) replace the remaining words with your own expressions; (5) write the summary out neatly.

## The Focus of Comprehension Questions

There have been several schemes to describe the possible focuses of comprehension questions (Tollefson, 1989; Day and Park, 2005). Typically they cover the following:

1. *Literal comprehension of the text.* This involves understanding what the text explicitly says. At their easiest, such questions could be answered by quoting parts of the text. These questions would be more demanding if the learners were not allowed to look at the text while answering the questions.
2. *Drawing inferences from the text.* This involves taking messages from the text that are not explicitly stated but which could be justified by reference to the text. This can involve working out the main idea of the text, looking at the organisation of the text, determining the writer's attitude to the topic, interpreting characters, and working out cause and effect and other conjunction relationships which might not be explicitly stated.
3. *Using the text for other purposes in addition to understanding.* This involves applying ideas from the text to solve problems, applying the ideas in the text to personal experience, comparing ideas in the text with other ideas from outside the text, imagining extensions of the text, and fitting the ideas in the text into a wider field as in a review of the literature.
4. *Responding critically to the text.* This involves considering the quality of the evidence in the text, evaluating the adequacy of the content of the text, evaluating the quality of expression and clarity of language of the text, expressing agreement or disagreement with the ideas in the text, and expressing satisfaction or dissatisfaction with the text.

The value in having a list of such focuses is that it allows teachers to check the questions they set their learners to see if they are providing a suitable range of focuses. Kraus-Srebrič et al. (1981) have shown that it is possible to devise comprehension activities for young learners at different levels of challenge using Bloom et al.'s (1956) six-level taxonomy. These six levels, starting from the least demanding, involve the focuses of knowledge, comprehension, application, analysis, synthesis, and evaluation, four of which are described above.

The above list of four focuses is roughly in order of difficulty and there is some evidence that more demanding questions involve deeper and more thoughtful processing and can result in more substantial language learning. Learners can also get involved in question making as the following techniques show.

In **predicting the passage** the learners see about eight topic-related words taken from a text they are going to read. They use these words to predict what sort of text it is and what content it will contain (Rinvolucri, 1981). Learners can also be encouraged to make questions rather than statements based on some starting point. Their reading attempts to find answers to those questions. The starting point for the questions can be: (1) the title or the first sentence of the text; (2) the theme of the text; (3) the pictures which accompany the text; (4) the previous parts of the text (Henry, 1984). The first sentence of a text can be used for predicting in the following ways (Nation, 1993).

1. The first sentence is used to decide what topic type the text is likely to be (see Chapter 9 for a discussion of topic types). As topic types are based on the general content matter of texts, this allows for very rich prediction. For example, a text beginning with the sentence "For this recipe, it is better to use fish that will not break up too easily" is likely to tell you how to do something. That is, it is an example of the instruction topic type. Texts which are of the instruction topic type typically tell you what tools and ingredients are needed, what steps to follow, what to be careful about at some of the steps and what the result of following the steps will be. It is surprisingly easy to guess the likely topic type from the first sentence and thus make very useful predictions.

2. The first sentence is used to predict what conjunction relationship might exist between the first sentence and the following sentence. Appendix 2 has a list of conjunction relationships—cause and effect, time sequence, contrast, etc. Often the first sentence will give a good clue of the following conjunction that could be inserted between it and the following sentence and this can suggest the rest of the paragraph. For example, "Independent reading is an activity in which children, alone or with friends, read their own self-selected books during a set period of time each day" (Smith and Elley, 1997: 41)

suggests that the next sentence(s) will amplify or provide more detail about independent reading.

3. The nouns in the first sentence are looked at to see which ones are indefinite nouns or noun groups. That is, which ones do not have specifying *the*, are indefinite plurals, begin with *a*, or are unspecified uncountable nouns. In the sentence on independent reading just quoted above, there are several indefinite noun groups—*independent reading* (an indefinite unaccountable noun), *an activity* (an indefinite countable noun with *a*), *children, friends* (indefinite plural nouns). Which of these indefinite nouns are likely to be specified or expanded on in the rest of the text?

Focusing on clues for prediction in this way applies the principle mentioned earlier, a good reading exercise directs the learners' attention to features of the text that can be found in almost any text. That is, studying today's text makes tomorrow's text easier.

Some words are written on the blackboard for the **guess the questions** activity. The learners are told that these words will be a part of questions and/or answers to questions based on the passage, but the teacher does not tell the learners what the questions will be. While the learners read they thus try to guess what the questions will be and find the answers. This is a very amusing technique and ensures a lot of close attention to the passage. When they finish reading, the teacher then gives the questions or asks the learners to tell him their guesses about the questions and asks for the answers. The teacher can either write all the suggested questions on the blackboard or just choose the questions that are the same as the ones he made. Here is an example based on the sample text on reading faster (Figure 3.1).

1. long      fixation
2. jump      time
3. pattern   fixation   jump

After the learners have read the passage and tried to guess the questions, the teacher asks them what they thought the questions were. The teacher then puts the real questions on the board and the learners answer them.

1. How long is the average fixation?
2. Does a jump take a long time?
3. What is a typical reading pattern?

In **group questions**, the learners are divided into small groups. Each group makes some questions based on the passage. Then the groups exchange questions and answer them. The groups mark each other's work.

The learners are divided into groups for **class questions**. If the passage is quite long, it is divided into parts. Each group makes some questions for a different part. Then the teacher asks the groups, one after another, to read out their questions. They are written on the blackboard and the class discusses them. Everybody answers all the questions.

## Standardised Reading Procedures

There are several examples of a range of techniques and strategies which are put together in an approach that is then given its own special name. These approaches are usually more than just a collection of strategies and include principles to guide the teaching and learning, and a theory that justifies the particular approach. Some of these approaches, such as reciprocal teaching and CORI, have been the focus of experimental research.

In the **standard reading exercise**, the learners are taught a series of questions to ask that can be used with any text. These questions can be taught in the learners' first language. Usually the questions cover what are thought to be the most important reading skills, such as predicting, choosing the main points, deciding on the writer's purpose, etc. (Edge, 1985; Scott, Carioni, Zanatta, Bayer and Quintanilha, 1984; Walker, 1987).

Palincsar and Brown (1986) designed a procedure called **reciprocal teaching** which involved the training and use of four strategies which could be applied paragraph by paragraph to the text: (1) prediction of the content of the paragraph before reading it; (2) making questions focusing on the main idea of the paragraph; (3) summarising what has just been read; and (4) seeking clarification on difficult points in the paragraph. The set of strategies has been called "reciprocal teaching" and the idea is that the procedure is modelled by the teacher and gradually taken over by the learners working in groups, and finally learners working independently.

Concept-oriented reading instruction (**CORI**) is an integrated strategy approach to reading comprehension (Guthrie, 2003). It involves systematic explicit instruction in the six strategies of activating background knowledge, questioning, searching for information, summarising, organising graphically, and structuring stories. The strategy instruction involves working through the sequence of modelling, scaffolding, and guided practice. Strategy practice should involve a minimum of 30 minutes per day.

## Vocabulary

Intensive reading can be an opportunity for teachers and learners to work on vocabulary. In the broad scheme of things, vocabulary work in intensive reading should make up only a very small proportion of the vocabulary development programme. Vocabulary teaching during intensive reading needs to share the time in the language-focused learning strand of a vocabulary programme with deliberate learning using word cards, vocabulary strategy training, and vocabulary teaching not related to intensive reading.

The following principles should guide attention to vocabulary in intensive reading.

1. High frequency words (words from the first 2,000 and Academic Word List) deserve sustained attention.
2. Low frequency words are best ignored or dealt with quickly.
3. The vocabulary learning strategies of guessing from context, analysing words using word parts, and dictionary use deserve repeated attention over a long period of time. These strategies can be practised with both high frequency and low frequency words.

The following options could be used during intensive reading (see Nation (2004a or 2008: Chapter 4) for a more detailed description).

*Techniques for High Frequency Vocabulary*

- Pre-teach a small amount of vocabulary from the passage before reading the passage. Such teaching must involve a reasonable amount of time on each word, focusing on several aspects of its form, meaning and use, such as its pronunciation, its word parts, its meaning, different senses of the word, common collocations, its grammar and any restrictions on its use, such as being technical, colloquial, impolite, etc.
- Put the word in an exercise after the text. Such exercises can include completing word family tables, matching words and meanings, classifying collocational patterns, and working out core meanings.
- Spend time on a word during the reading looking at several aspects of its form, meaning and use.
- Make a glossary before the learners read the text. The glossary is there to help learn the words.

*Techniques for Low Frequency Vocabulary*

- Ignore the word.
- Quickly give the meaning of the word by using a translation, picture, diagram, demonstration, or L2 definition.
- Replace the word in the text with a more useful high frequency word before the learners work on the text. Simplifying the text aims to reduce the density of unknown words so that the text is more accessible for the learners.

- Make a glossary before the learners see the text so that the learners can see the meanings of low frequency words, thus avoiding the need to spend valuable class time on them. Here the glossary has the role of getting rid of the need to pay attention to the word.

*Strategy-focused Techniques for High Frequency and Low Frequency Vocabulary*

- Help learners use context clues to guess the meaning of the word. The main goal of this is to practise and refine the guessing from context strategy.
- Help learners break a word into parts and relate the meaning of its parts to the meaning of the word. The main goal of this is to practise the word part strategy.
- Help learners use a dictionary to look up the meaning of a word and to gather extra information about the word so as to make it stay in their memory.

When the three strategies of guessing, word parts and dictionary use are practised with high frequency words, there is a bonus—a useful strategy is practised and a useful high frequency word may be learned. When the strategies are used with low frequency words, the teacher's main concern should be for the learning of the strategy (Nation, 2001).

By combining exercises that the learners have practised before, **part of speech, What does what?** and **conjunction relationships,** it is possible to guess the meanings of most new words from their context. The **guessing from context** strategy has five steps. They will be applied to the word *fixation* in the text in Figure 3.1.

- Step 1—Decide what part of speech the word is in the passage. (*fixation* is a noun)
- Step 2—Do the **What does what?** exercise with the word. If it is an adjective, for example <u>remote</u>, ask "What is <u>remote</u>?" If it is an adverb, for example <u>cosmically</u>, ask "What does what or what is what <u>cosmically</u>?" (A skilled reader makes around 95 fixations per 100 words)
- Step 3—See if the word is involved in any conjunction relationship. (*fixation* is related to *When people read,* and is one of *three types of action*)
- Step 4—Guess the meaning of the word. (look at something, keep looking, stop)
- Step 5—Check your guess by seeing that it is the same part of speech as the word in the passage, by checking for any prefixes, roots, or suffixes that will confirm your guess is correct or that might cause

you to guess again, and by substituting your guess for the word in the passage to see that it makes sense (Nation, 2001: 256–260).

This is a very useful vocabulary focused strategy.

### Grammar Features in the Text

Many learners expect grammar to get some attention in a language course. Focusing on grammar features during intensive reading provides a good opportunity to satisfy this expectation and at the same time to deal with grammar in a meaningful context. Most of the following activities involve focusing on the grammar to get a clear interpretation of a grammatically complex part of the text.

The following principles should guide attention to grammar in intensive reading.

1. High frequency grammar items deserve sustained attention. In general, such items tend to be formally simple. That is, the shorter a grammatical feature, the more frequent it is likely to be. Although frequency information about grammatical features has been around for a long time (George, 1963), it is only recently that grammar descriptions have included such information (Biber, Johansson, Leech, Conrad and Finegan, 1999).

2. Low frequency grammatical features are best given attention as part of strategies for dealing with complicated grammatical features such as subordinate clauses, coordination, and complicated noun groups. All of the following activities in this section on grammar are strategy based.

For the **part of speech** activity, the teacher chooses words from the passage and writes them with their line numbers on the blackboard. The learners find each word in the passage and say whether it is a noun, a verb, an adjective, or an adverb by writing n., v., adj., or adv. after it. The words chosen for this exercise are usually words that can be different parts of speech in different contexts. Being able to recognise the part of speech of a word in a given context has three values. First, when trying to guess the meaning of a word from the context, knowing the part of speech of the word will make sure that the meaning guessed is the same part of speech. Second, it makes looking up the word in a dictionary much easier because the meanings of words are usually classified according to the part of speech of the word. Third, if a sentence is difficult to understand, it might be because the learners are applying the wrong meaning or function to one or more of the words in the sentence. By checking the part of speech of the words the learners may be able to understand the sentence.

The **What does what?** exercise makes the learners look for the noun-verb relationships that are often not clearly seen because of the word order of a passage. The learners need to ask themselves the question "What does what?" or "What is what?" in order to see these relationships. The exercise becomes more difficult if the subject or object of a verb is separated from the verb by a clause, or if the verb is acting as a noun or adjective.

The teacher chooses verbs, or words related to verbs, from the passage and writes the list of words with line numbers on the blackboard. The learners find these words in the passage and write the subjects and objects (if any) of the words according to the passage. All the verbs should be written as active verbs.

Independent reading is an activity in which children, alone or with friends, read their own self-selected books during a set period of time each day. It is similar to the recreational reading done by adults, and provides a time for children to enjoy reading and to practise the skills learned in guided reading sessions.

(Smith and Elley, 1997: 41)

The exercise usually takes this form.

(line 2) read
(line 2) select
(line 4) provide
(line 4) enjoy
(line 4) practise

When learners write their answers, they must not use passives (they must make them active) and reference words like *it, he, they, this* must be replaced by what they refer to. So, to do the second item *select* above, the learners need to answer *children select their own books*. This exercise is very easy for the teacher to make, makes the learners look closely at the text, and is a useful way of focusing on features like nominalisation, clauses occurring after the subject, and coordination which can make reading difficult. **What does what?** can be a good substitute for comprehension questions.

The **coordination** activity involves simplifying sentences. Often when there is *and, but,* or *or* in a sentence, there are two parts of the sentence that are similar to each other and these parts may relate to some common part of the sentence. So in the sentence *The Earth is a planet just under 8,000 miles in diameter, moving round the Sun at a distance of 93,000,000 miles, and completing one circuit in 365¼ day*s, moving around the sun at a distance of 93,000,000 miles and completing one circuit in 365¼ days are parallel. They both relate to the common part The Earth is a planet just under 8,000 miles in diameter. So, the sentence can be rewritten as two separate sentences, *The Earth is a planet just under 8,000 miles in diameter, moving round the Sun at a distance of 93,000,000 miles* and *The Earth is a planet just under 8,000 miles in diameter completing one circuit in 365¼ days.* Where the items joined by <u>and</u>, <u>but</u>, or <u>or</u> are short, it is not worth rewriting the sentence when answering the exercise. Instead, the similar parts can be underlined and numbered.

The teacher writes the line numbers of *and, but* or *or* on the whiteboard, for example:

(line 20)     *and*

The learners have to mark the parallel parts or rewrite the sentence as two or more sentences. If learners find the exercise difficult, it can be broken into the following steps.

1. Find <u>and</u>, <u>but</u> or <u>or</u>.
2. Look at what follows.
3. Find a similar part of speech in front of <u>and</u>, <u>but</u> or <u>or</u>.
4. Decide what part of the sentence (if any) the similar parts relate to.
5. Rewrite the sentence so that each sentence contains the common part plus one of the similar parts.

This exercise is one step in the strategy of simplifying complicated sentences.

**Simplifying noun groups**, like the coordination activity, involves looking for the essence of a sentence. Noun groups containing items following the headword of the group add considerably to the difficulty of a sentence. Here are some examples from the sample text on reading speed. The headword in the noun group has been underlined.

three <u>types</u> of action
<u>movements</u> back to an item already looked at
an <u>item</u> already looked at
the maximum <u>number</u> of letters that can be seen clearly in one fixation

This exercise teaches the learners to find these parts and thus makes it easier to see the overall plan of the sentence. The learners number the items following the headword simply to make themselves conscious of the forms these items can take so that they will recognise them more readily. This exercise is one step in simplifying sentences. It is also useful for understanding reference words because once the head noun referred to has been found, it is still necessary to find the beginning and end of that noun group.

The teacher chooses the headwords of noun groups from the passage and writes the list of headwords with line numbers on the whiteboard.

| (line 1) | types |
| (line 1) | fixations |
| (line 3) | movements |
| (line 13) | number |
| (line 17) | average |

The learners find these words in the passage, circle them, and draw a bracket "(" at the beginning of the noun group and another bracket ")" at the end. If the noun group contains words which come after the headword, the learners show what form these following words take by writing a number according to the list given below. Here are the seven kinds of items that may typically follow the headword of a noun group, with examples. The headword has been underlined and the following items are in italics.

1. a preposition + a noun (their own special <u>points</u> *of interest*)
2. <u>who</u>, <u>that</u>, <u>which</u> etc. + a clause (the only two <u>planets</u> *which do not appear overwhelmingly hostile*)
3. stem + ing (a <u>planet</u> . . . *completing one circuit in 365 days*)
4. stem + ed (a contact <u>lens</u> *manufactured to a preconceived formula*)
5. to + stem (the first contact <u>lenses</u> *to enjoy wide use amongst the general public*)
6. a noun in apposition (our one natural <u>satellite</u>, *the moon*)
7. an adjective (the <u>stars</u> *visible at night-time*)

*A Sentence Simplification Strategy*

By combining exercises that they have practised before, **reference words**, **coordination**, **simplifying noun groups**, and **What does what?** learners can simplify sentences that seem to be too complicated for them to understand. The strategy has four steps.

- Step 1—Find the reference words in the difficult sentence and find what they refer to.
- Step 2—Rewrite the sentences as two or more sentences by removing <u>and</u>, <u>but</u>, or <u>or</u>.
- Step 3—Find the nouns and remove the items following the nouns which are a part of each noun group.
- Step 4—Do the **What does what?** exercise with the verbs to make sure their subjects and objects are known.

The learners should memorise the steps of this strategy so they can apply it whenever they meet a difficult sentence.

If the sentence *Of course, the nearest to us are Mars, which may approach the Earth to within 35,000,000 miles, and Venus, which has a minimum distance from us of only about 24,000,000 miles.* was simplified according to these steps, the result would be

*Of course the nearest are    Mars    and    Venus*

## Cohesive Devices

The classic text on cohesion is Halliday and Hasan (1976) *Cohesion in English*. Their categorisation of the major cohesive devices is the model for the following activities. The arguments for focusing on cohesive devices are that they occur in every text so the learning from one text should readily transfer to the reading of another text, and that they focus learners' attention on the message of the text at a level beyond the sentence level. Cohesion involves the devices of reference words, substitution and ellipsis, comparison, conjunction relationships, and lexical cohesion. Exercises focusing on cohesive devices are easy to make and the discussion of the answers can lead to useful insights into language use that can have positive effects on both reading and writing.

### Reference Words and Substitutes

Reference words include words like *he, she, his, her, this, that, these, those, it, its,* and *which*. Substitutes consist of *so, one(s), the same* and *not*. For the purpose of this reading exercise it is not necessary to distinguish between reference and substitution although Halliday and Hasan (1976: Chapters 2 and 3) have shown that there are important differences between them. This exercise helps learners recognise some of the signals that show that a sentence is related to something that has been mentioned elsewhere in the text.

Each reference word or substitute has its own grammar and when learners have difficulty understanding these words in a context, this grammar should be used as the basis for preparation before the exercise, and for discussion when marking. *Their*, for example, can only refer to plural nouns or two or more related singular nouns. *This* can refer to singular nouns, to a phrase, a clause, or a group of clauses or sentences. *He* usually refers to a singular, male person. *They* cannot have singular reference.

The exercise can take this form. The teacher writes the reference word on the blackboard with its line number next to it (see Figure 3.1, page 31).

*it* (line 7)
*these* (line 10)
*this* (line 13)

The learners copy their answer from the text and give the line number of their answer. The learners can check their answers by making sure the grammar of their answer agrees with the grammar of the reference word and by substituting the words referred to for the reference word to see that the sentence containing the reference word makes sense. The exercise on noun groups in the grammar section of this chapter helps with this exercise because often the reference word refers to a noun plus other items in the noun group. The exercise may also be done as a multiple-choice exercise (Mackay and Mountford, 1976).

*Ellipsis*

Ellipsis occurs when something which is structurally necessary is left unsaid. What is left unsaid is usually recoverable from a previous part of the passage. Ellipsis is very common in dialogue but it is also found in some written texts, as in the following example.

> *Most words are fixated on, but function words much less often than content words.*

Exercises on ellipsis help learners make sense of sentences by giving them practice in recovering the missing parts. The easiest type of exercise tells the learner where there is ellipsis.

> (line 6) What happens *less often*?

The exercise can also take the form of a question. What is missing from this sentence? Rewrite the sentence as a complete sentence.

Ellipsis can also occur when two clauses are coordinated with *and*. The beginning of the second clause may be left out because it is the same as the beginning of the first clause. Here is an example.

> It is similar to the recreational reading done by adults, and provides a time for children to enjoy reading <u>and</u> to practice the skills learned in guided reading sessions (Smith and Elley, 1999: 41).

*Comparison*

Halliday and Hasan (1976) include much of comparison under reference. Words used in comparison include <u>same</u>, <u>similar</u>, <u>identical</u>, <u>equal</u>, <u>different</u>, <u>other</u>, <u>additional</u>, <u>else</u>, <u>likewise</u>, <u>so</u>, <u>more</u>, <u>fewer</u>, <u>less</u>, adjectives or adverbs + -<u>er</u>. Often comparison between sentences and this type of exercise helps the learners understand the passage by helping them to see what is being compared. The exercise can take this form.

> <u>others</u>. Other than what?
> <u>farther</u> than what?
> <u>smaller, thinner, and lighter</u> than what?

In another form, the comparison word with its line number is written on the blackboard. The learners write the two things that are compared.

*Conjunction Relationships*

Signals of conjunction like <u>and</u>, <u>namely</u>, <u>but</u>, <u>in spite of this</u>, relate sentences or parts of sentences to each other. Generally speaking, they show "the way in which what is to follow is systematically connected to what has gone before" (Halliday and Hasan, 1976: 227). The list of types of conjunction relationships in Appendix 2 is complete enough for teaching reading. Knowing about conjunction relationships has five useful effects.

1. It helps the learners to see how ideas in a passage are related to each other and to discover the effect of a statement on other parts of the text.
2. It helps in finding the meanings of words in context. If, for example, an unknown word occurs in the effect clause of a cause–effect relationship, then it is possible to find the meaning of that word because the effect can be guessed from the cause.
3. It is important in finding the main idea in a paragraph. Effects are usually more important than causes. The second item in a contrast is more important than the first. The weightings in column 4 in Appendix 2 show this.
4. It helps in learning new connectives. For example, *moreover* signals the inclusion relationship. Knowing this simplifies learning the meaning of *moreover*.
5. It helps in predicting what will come in a passage.

Exercises on conjunction may draw attention to the signals of conjunction which include: conjunctions *so*, *because*, *while*; adverbs *firstly*, *however*, *alternatively*; verbs *cause*, *follow*, *exemplify*; preposition groups and other forms. However, many sentences are in a conjunction relationship which is not formally signalled at all. Thus it is the relationship between the two clauses which is most important and which should be given most attention. Here are three types of conjunction exercise in increasing order of difficulty (see Figure 3.1, page 31 for the text).

1. *Because* (line 20) signals a cause-effect relationship. What is the cause? What is the effect?
2. Find the following words in the passage. Say what relationship each one signals and find the two related parts.

   *When*   (line 1)
   *but*     (line 5)
   *thus*    (line 21)

3. What relationship occurs in lines 5–6? What is the signal, if any? What are the two parts?

*Lexical Cohesion*

Halliday and Hasan (1976: 278) distinguish repetition, synonyms, near synonyms, superordinates, and general words. These are all used to refer to exactly the same item in the passage. Thus, in a passage about Thomas Telford, he is referred to as *Tom, their son, the baby, the boy, Thomas*. Obviously it is important for the reader to realise that a change in the noun used does not necessarily mean a change in the person being referred to.

1. What does *all* (line 17) in the passage (Figure 3.1) refer to?
2. What different words are used in the passage to refer to *words*?

## Genre Features

Intensive reading is a good opportunity for making learners aware of how the various vocabulary, grammatical, cohesive, formatting, and ideas content aspects of a text work together to achieve the communicative purpose of the text. A useful introduction to this is the predicting activity where learners use the topic and first sentence to predict what a text will be about. Here is an example from Nation (1993). The title of the text is *Limestone Caves*, and the first sentence is "Limestone is just one of the many kinds of rocks found in New Zealand". To predict what will occur in the following text, the learners can draw on several generalisable systems of knowledge. These include features that we have looked at earlier in this chapter— grammatical features (particularly verb forms and noun groups), conjunction relationships, and topic types. Here is how it can be done. The first sentence mentioned above contains the verb *is* which is present tense. This suggests it is likely to be about a general description rather than a particular event. The first sentence contains indefinite noun groups, that is, noun groups without the definite article *the* or some other specifier. These nouns are *limestone* and *rocks*. One or both of these indefinite noun groups is likely to be described in detail in the following text, probably *limestone*. We could also ask what kind of conjunction relationship is likely to exist between the first sentence and the following sentence. If we look at the list in Appendix 2, the most likely candidate is amplification. That is sentence 2 and perhaps the rest of the passage will give us more detail about something in the first sentence. The third system of knowledge we can use for predicting is topic type (see Chapter 9). This text seems likely to tell us what something is like. The title *Limestone Caves* (an indefinite noun group) indicates that. So it is likely to be an example of the characteristics topic type. The characteristics topic type includes the features of the thing described of them (limestone caves), proof that some of the features exist such as examples, the general category that the thing fits into, and other information about the thing. We should thus expect at least some of these kinds of information to occur in the paragraph or text.

## Handling the Exercises

Most of the exercises described in this chapter have one important feature in common. They do not require specially constructed or adapted texts. They can be applied to any texts that the teacher has or to texts that the learners use in their study of other subjects. Moreover, the exercises do not require a large amount of preparation. The exercises can be written up quickly on the blackboard and the learners can use some type of coding system to mark them on their texts, underlining for reference words, a box around a word for part of speech, and so on.

Each exercise is like a test, but it should be clear to the learners what feature they are looking at and the significance of this feature for reading. Each exercise requires certain types of knowledge which can be specified. Thus, when learners make an error, or before they do the exercise, the teacher or the learners in groups can go through the knowledge needed to do the exercise.

## The Role of Teaching Exercises

The focus in this chapter has been on language-focused learning activities that teach rather than just provide practice. Exercises that teach are used in the belief that through such teaching, learning will be faster and more sure. Such exercises have an obvious value where time is short or where learners have not succeeded in learning to read well by other methods. But these exercises are not a substitute for practice. It is very important that learners should have the opportunity to gain meaning-focused input through reading plenty of material that does not contain too many unknown or difficult items. This meaning-focused input material provides the learners with experience in reading and allows them to apply what they have learned in other parts of the reading course.

They should also have the opportunity to work with very easy material so that they can develop fluency in reading. These two points are taken up in the following chapter on extensive reading.

CHAPTER **4**

# Extensive Reading

Extensive reading fits into the meaning-focused input and fluency development strands of a course, depending on the level of the books that the learners read. When the books contain only a few unknown vocabulary and grammar items, extensive reading provides the conditions for meaning-focused input. Where the books are very easy ones with virtually no unknown items, extensive reading provides the conditions for fluency development.

This chapter examines the research on graded readers to draw up a set of guidelines for setting up and managing extensive reading programmes. These guidelines involve understanding the type of learning that can occur through such reading, determining learners' existing vocabulary knowledge, having interesting and engaging books, getting learners to do large quantities of reading, and making sure that the learning from reading is supported by other kinds of learning. In order to meet the conditions needed for learning from extensive reading at a variety of levels of proficiency, it is essential to make use of simplified texts.

Reading is a source of learning and a source of enjoyment. It can be a goal in its own right and a way of reaching other goals. As a source of learning, reading can establish previously learned vocabulary and grammar, it can help learners learn new vocabulary and grammar, and through success in language use it can encourage learners to learn more and continue with their language study. As a goal in its own right, reading can be a source of enjoyment and a way of gaining knowledge of the world. As learners gain skill and fluency in reading, their enjoyment can increase.

However, because of the nature of reading and learning from reading, a reading development programme will benefit from careful planning and monitoring. There are two major language-based reasons for this. First, reading requires considerable knowledge and skill. This knowledge includes recognising the letters and words of the language, having a large vocabulary and substantial grammatical and textual knowledge, being able to bring knowledge of the world to the reading task, and developing a degree of fluency with the reading skill. Second, learning through extensive reading is largely incidental learning, that is, the learners' attention is focused on the story not on items to learn. As a result, learning gains tend to be fragile and thus it is important to have quantity of input with substantial opportunities for vocabulary repetition.

This quantity of input needs to be close to 500,000 running words per year, which is equivalent to 25 graded readers a year, or one and a half substantial first year university textbooks, or six unsimplified novels. This needs to continue over several years. In the following discussion of planning and running an extensive reading programme, we will look at the conditions for learning that need to exist, the quantities of text that learners need to read, how to keep learners motivated, and the principles that teachers should follow in running the programme. The chapter is organised around a set of guidelines for planning a programme.

## Understand the Goals and Limitations of Extensive Reading

Extensive reading is a form of learning from meaning-focused input. During extensive reading learners should be interested in what they are reading and should be reading with their attention on the meaning of the text rather than on learning the language features of the text. Extensive reading can occur within class time (Elley and Mangubhai, 1981), or outside class time. In their very useful survey of extensive reading, Day and Bamford (1998) characterise extensive reading as involving a large quantity of varied, self-selected, enjoyable reading at a reasonably fluent speed.

There is now plenty of evidence (Elley, 1991) that reading can result in a variety of substantial proficiency gains. However, it is important to note that these gains require considerable time and effort. In their classic study of extensive reading, Elley and Mangubhai (1981) had 8 to 10-year-old learners read in class time for no more than 30 minutes per day each school day for almost eight months. The results were remarkable with learners making the equivalent of 15 months' gain in eight months. However, the time involved was substantial, but not beyond the means of an English as a foreign language situation.

In a study of learners reading a single graded reading text, Waring and

Takaki (2003) used vocabulary tests at three levels of difficulty (Which of these words did you meet in the text?, a multiple-choice test, and a translation test) to measure vocabulary learning. The three tests all involved the same 25 words. These three tests represented different levels of vocabulary knowledge. On the word form recognition test, the learners scored 15.3 out of 25, on the multiple-choice test 10.6, and on the translation test 4.6. These results show that only a small number of words (4.6 out of 25) were learned well, but a much larger number (up to 15 out of 25) had taken a useful step towards being known. Further meetings with these words should strengthen and enrich this knowledge. The Waring and Takaki study included a delayed post-test which showed that over a period of time without further reinforcement, the vocabulary gains from reading were gradually lost. It is thus important to make sure that there are repeated opportunities to meet the same vocabulary in reading, and these repeated opportunities should not be delayed too long. Teachers considering setting up an extensive reading programme should understand very clearly that such a programme needs to involve large amounts of reading and needs to continue for a long time. If this happens, the results will be impressive.

## Find Your Learners' Present Vocabulary Level

Extensive reading can only occur if 95 to 98 percent of the running words in a text are already familiar to the learner or are no burden to the learner (Hu and Nation, 2000). Hu and Nation investigated learners' comprehension of a fiction text at different levels of known word density. Where only 80 percent of the running words were known, no learners gained adequate comprehension. Where 90 or 95 percent of the words were known, a few learners gained adequate comprehension but the majority did not. The degree of comprehension was predictable from the density of unknown words and the optimum density was 98 percent. That is, no more than two words in every 100 running words should be unfamiliar to the reader. This estimate is probably conservative because research with native speakers (Carver, 1994) indicates that a density of 99 percent is preferable for meaning-focused input. If we relate these densities to the vocabulary size needed to read an unsimplified fiction text, we find that learners would need a vocabulary of 9,000 words to read novels written for adults (Nation, 2006). The clear message from this is that for learners of English to do extensive reading at the elementary and intermediate stages of proficiency, it is essential that they read graded readers that have been specially prepared for learners of English. It is only by reading such texts that learners can have the density of known words that is essential for extensive reading.

Graded readers typically cover a range of levels beginning at around

300–500 words and going to around 2,000–2,500 words. For example, there are six vocabulary levels in the Oxford Bookworms series.

| Level | New words | Cumulative words |
|---|---|---|
| 1 | 400 | 400 |
| 2 | 300 | 700 |
| 3 | 300 | 1,000 |
| 4 | 400 | 1,400 |
| 5 | 400 | 1,800 |
| 6 | 700 | 2,500 |

In order to know at what level learners should begin reading, it is useful to measure their receptive vocabulary size. This involves measuring their knowledge of the most frequent 2,000 words of English. The test developed by Schmitt, Schmitt and Clapham (2001) provides a means of doing this. There are also very useful bilingual vocabulary tests which can be used to do this (see the Vocabulary Resource Booklet at http://www.vuw.ac.nz/lals/staff/paul-nation/nation.aspx).

### Provide Plenty of Interesting and Appropriate Reading Texts

We have looked briefly at the Oxford Bookworms series. This is an excellent and well established series of graded readers with many interesting titles. However, it is only one of many series of readers that are available (see Hill, 1997, 2001; Thomas and Hill, 1993; Hill and Thomas, 1988 and 1989 for reviews). Hill (in Day and Bamford, 1998) says that there are around 1,650 graded readers in print. These are in over 40 different series. Unfortunately, the levels in these series are not identical with each other in the number of levels, the amount of vocabulary at each level, nor the vocabulary lists on which they are based. This is not as serious as it sounds. There seems to be quite a big overlap between the vocabulary covered in the different series, and any particular reader can only make use of some of the words available at a particular level.

It is thus not important to stick to only one series of graded readers. It is much better to choose titles from any of the available series that are interesting and well written. Hill (in Day and Bamford, 1998) provides a very useful list of what he considers to be the best graded readers and this is a very valuable starting point in building a collection of graded readers. As there is no recent report of what learners enjoy most, it is worth collecting data on this. The Extensive Reading Foundation website (http://www.erfoundation.org/) is also an excellent source of award-winning graded reader titles.

If an extensive reading programme is to be successful, it must provide books that learners are interested in reading or that will develop their interest in reading. Teachers' judgements of books are likely to be different from learners' judgements of books, and learners' judgements should get priority.

## Set, Encourage and Monitor Large Quantities of Extensive Reading

Research on the vocabulary covered by different numbers of graded readers (Nation and Wang, 1999) suggests that learners need to read many books in order to gain control of the high frequency words of English, preferably at the rate of a graded reader every one or two weeks. There are several techniques and procedures that can be used to motivate learners to do this and to keep a record of their reading.

In an extensive reading programme, reading should be the main activity and other activities should occupy only a very small proportion of the time so that time is not taken away from reading. For this reason, most extensive reading programmes do not require learners to do elaborate comprehension tests or exercises on the books they read. Generally, learners are simply required to fill out a short record form indicating the name of the book they have just read, its level, the date, how long it took to read, and a brief comment on the quality of the book (Was it a good story? Would you recommend it to others?). Twelve or more of these short report forms can be printed on one piece of A4 paper, allowing the learner and teacher to see at a glance how much has been read over what period of time.

Additional activities to motivate reading may take a bit more time. There may be a slip of paper in the back of each book for learners to record their opinion of the book. Other learners considering whether to choose to read this book could look at this slip of paper to see what others thought of it.

**Oral book reports** involve a learner presenting a commentary on a book to the class or a reading group. The idea behind such reports is not to give away the story of the book but to encourage others to read it. These reports can follow a set format covering questions like what was the name of the book, what type of story was it (a mystery, a love story, etc.), where and when was it set, was it enjoyable, who would like to read it?

**Discussion groups** can bring learners together who have already all read the same book. Such a group should consist of four or five learners. As a result of their discussion, they may prepare an oral book report or a written review to present to others in the class. They then decide what book they will discuss at their next meeting.

The Extensive Reading Foundation has been set up to recognise quality in the production of graded readers. Awards are given to the best books each year just like the Oscars for movies.

After the extensive reading programme has been running for some time, learners can vote on what they thought were the best books they read. Labels can be stuck on the front of the winning books to indicate that they are well worth reading.

As well as books getting awards, learners can get awards for the quantity of reading that they do. After reading five books an award can be given, and after ten a further award, and so on.

The way books are displayed can encourage reading. Publishers now try to make graded readers as attractive as possible with colourful covers sometimes showing a scene from the movie based on the book. Displays can be arranged to show the different types of stories, the range of levels, new books, and books that have won awards or have been highly recommended.

The aim of all these activities is to keep learners excited about reading and wanting to read more.

## Support and Supplement Extensive Reading with Language-focused Learning and Fluency Development

An extensive reading programme is only one part of a language course. Teachers need to make sure that other parts of the course are supporting extensive reading and that extensive reading is supporting other parts of the course.

One of the most useful ways in which the course can support extensive reading is by providing training in reading faster. A speed reading programme involves the learners reading texts that are well within their language knowledge; that is, they contain no unknown vocabulary or grammatical features. Their reading of each text is timed, and their speed and comprehension scores are recorded on graphs so that learners can easily see their progress and are encouraged to increase their reading speed. Properly designed courses are usually very successful with most learners soon doubling their speed. A good reading speed is around 250 words per minute. Most learners without training read at less that 100 words per minute. The essential requirements for such a course are: (1) easy texts (Quinn, Nation and Millett, 2007; Millett, 2005 Books 1 and 2; Nation and Malarcher, 2007); (2) regular practice (about three times a week); and (3) a push to read faster (see Chapter 5).

One way an extensive reading programme can contribute to proficiency development is through vocabulary growth. This can be encouraged in extensive reading by making the vocabulary learning more deliberate and less incidental. Care needs to be taken, however, that this vocabulary learning goal does not overshadow reading for pleasure. Here are some brief suggestions that may boost vocabulary learning from extensive reading.

1. Before reading a text, the learner quickly skims it and selects five or six words to focus on while reading. This has the effect of raising consciousness about some words and thus making them more noticeable when they are met again in the text.
2. While reading the learner can collect new words that are repeated in the text to put on word cards for later deliberate study.
3. A more formal follow up to this is for learners to report to the class on a word that they met while reading—explaining what it means, how it was used in the text, its word parts, its etymology, and any unusual features about it.
4. The use of a dictionary while reading should also have positive effects (Knight, 1994), although this tends to increase the time it takes to read a text (Hulstijn, 1993).

After reading a graded reader, the learner can spend a few minutes reflecting on new words that were met in the book and looking back in the book to revise them.

Vocabulary learning and reading are helped if the learners are good at guessing the meanings of unknown words from context clues. Guessing from context is a trainable strategy and it is worth spending a few minutes on it each week. There are several ways of practising the strategy, but all require a text where there is not a heavy density of unknown words. Typically, the teacher should model the procedure for the learners, then work together with the learners on some items, then get the learners working together in pairs and eventually working individually.

A deductive guessing procedure involves the learners making a guess at the meaning of an unknown word in a text and then justifying their guesses. This involves a discussion of the various available clues.

An inductive guessing procedure involves looking at the available clues—the part of speech of the unknown word, its immediate context, and the relationship between the clause with the unknown word and the adjoining clauses (for a detailed description, see Nation, 2001; Nation, 2008). It is worth spending small amounts of time over several weeks or months on practising guessing because it is a very powerful and useful strategy.

## Help Learners Move Systematically Through the Graded Reader Levels

Research on the occurrence of vocabulary in graded readers can provide useful guidelines for planning such reading. Nation and Wang (1999), in a detailed study of 42 graded readers in the Oxford Bookworms series, reached the following conclusions, considering only the aim of vocabulary learning.

1. Learners should read at least one graded reader every week, no matter what level they are reading at. This rate of reading allows unknown vocabulary to be repeated before the immediately previous occurrence is forgotten.
2. Learners should read at least five books at a level (say Level 2) before moving to books at the next level (Level 3). This number of books provides a chance for most of the vocabulary introduced at that level to occur.
3. Learners should read more books at the later levels than the earlier. This is because the vocabulary of the earlier levels occurs very frequently in the books at the later levels. Books at the later levels thus provide good conditions for learning all the vocabulary of the graded reader series.
4. Learners should read at least 15–20 and preferably 30 readers in a year. This number of graded readers provides plenty of repetition for the vocabulary and provides the opportunity to meet most of the vocabulary several times. A programme where learners read only three or four graded readers per year is not an extensive reading programme.
5. Learners should work their way through the levels of graded readers as the later levels provide excellent conditions for establishing the vocabulary of the earlier levels.
6. Learners may need to study directly the new vocabulary at the earlier levels or at least make use of a dictionary when starting to read books at a particular level. This is because the density of unknown vocabulary tends to be a little higher at the earlier levels.

Extensive reading programmes do not run as neatly as the guidelines described above. Learners often choose books according to their appeal without considering the level of the reader. So they may read a Level 2 reader, then a Level 5 reader, then a Level 3 reader, and so on. This does not matter too much as long as plenty of enjoyable reading is done. An extensive reading programme needs to have a fluency strand (where learners read very easy texts quickly) and a meaning-focused input strand (where learners read with around 98 percent coverage). It also does not hurt if there is occasional language-focused learning through extensive reading where learners struggle through an interesting but difficult text. Moving around the levels provides these different levels of opportunities for learning. Some learners begin reading with enthusiasm and then stall when they see that the reading takes time and effort. Some learners have great trouble getting started. Others read very slowly and laboriously and are reluctant to increase their reading speed. All of these problems have solutions and teachers need to monitor learners' progress carefully by looking at their record sheets, observing them while they are reading, and talking with them individually about their goals, progress and problems. When learners are not enthusiastic readers, it helps initially to make extensive reading part of the programme during class time, with the teacher ensuring that the reading is done. When learners become hooked on reading, it can then be set as an out-of-class activity.

## Simplified and Unsimplified Texts

For some teachers and researchers, graded readers are seen as being inauthentic, watered-down versions of richer original texts. Vocabulary simplification is also seen to result in more complicated grammar as what could be neatly expressed in one word is now expressed in several simpler words. These criticisms are largely true of the poorest quality graded readers but there are many of high quality (Day and Bamford, 1998).

Publishers and editors of graded readers would say that the most convincing argument in favour of graded readers is that there are numerous interesting well-written books, many of them not simplifications but original language-learner literature. This is undoubtedly true. From a vocabulary learning perspective, however, the most convincing argument is that the vocabulary control required by the graded reader schemes results in texts where there are very few low frequency words and the high frequency words of the language get plenty of repetition. As a contrast, let us compare a simplified version of *Dracula* (written within a 700-word vocabulary at Level 2 of the Oxford Bookworms series) and the original version (Nation and Deweerdt, 2001).

Table 4.1 shows that the books differ greatly in length. The simplified version is much shorter than the original. The coverage by the first two thousand words and proper nouns shows how accessible each book would

**Table 4.1** A Comparison of the Vocabulary in the Simplified and Original Versions of *Dracula*

|  | Simplified version | Original |
| --- | --- | --- |
| Length of the books | 7,957 words | 161,425 words |
| Percentage coverage by the first 2,000 words of English plus proper nouns | 98.6% | 92.8% |
| Total word families | 556 | 5,640 |
| Number of word families not in the first 2,000 occurring only once in the book | 19 | 3,038 |

be for a learner with a limited vocabulary. Proper nouns are included because these do not need to be known before reading the text. Coverage of 98.6% means that there is just over one unknown word in every 100. Coverage of 92.8% means that there are just over seven unknown words in every 100, or almost one in every line of the text. This is a heavy vocabulary load.

The total number of word families in the book is another indication of how accessible the book would be to a learner with a limited vocabulary. This figure is directly affected by the different lengths of the books, but even if the lengths were the same, the number of word families in the simplified version would be much less than in the original (the first 7,957 running words of the original *Dracula* contains 1,435 word families). The most striking contrast, however, is in the number of words occurring only once in the books. The original version has a very large number and when we look at the kinds of words that make up this number, it is easy to see how difficult and unrewarding it would be for an elementary or intermediate language learner to try to read such books. Here are some of the 3,038 words that only occur once in the original of *Dracula—solicitude, therapeutics, physiognomy, mundane, lugubrious.* If these words were looked up in a dictionary while reading, they would not help with later parts of the text because they occur only once. They are also likely to be forgotten before they are met again in other texts. Eventually, advanced learners may need to learn these words, but they should be learned when the more useful high frequency words are already very well known. Unsimplified texts have a very heavy vocabulary load and, for the purposes of extensive reading, do not set up the conditions needed for successful learning from meaning-focused input. *Dracula*, in spite of its age, is typical of other unsimplified texts, including recent unsimplified texts written for teenagers.

## Other Ways of Supporting Extensive Reading

Not all texts for extensive reading need to be simplified texts as there are other ways of helping with the vocabulary load of extensive reading. These include glossing, computer-assisted reading, and elaborating.

### Glossing

**Glossing** involves providing the meanings of words in L1 or in a simple L2 definition in the margin next to the line containing an unknown word. Some glossaries come at the end of a text, but learners prefer glosses near the unknown word, probably because these do not disrupt reading too much. In Japan, some English texts are printed with translations in a lighter type above the low frequency word in the text. Glosses may contribute to vocabulary learning and may improve comprehension of the text, although the research on this is not conclusive. Glosses are an alternative to dictionary use and are generally less disruptive than dictionaries. Using dictionaries while reading usually adds considerably to the time taken to complete reading the text. There is renewed interest in research on glossing as a result of the growth in computer-assisted reading.

## Computer-assisted Reading

One of the best **computer-assisted reading** programs can be found on Tom Cobb's website www.lextutor.ca. Look under the heading *Read with resources.* The learner pastes in a text, clicks *build,* and then starts reading. By clicking once on a word, a spoken form of the word can be heard. By clicking twice, several concordance examples appear. These additional contexts can help with guessing the word's meaning from context clues. By clicking on a dictionary link, the word can be looked up in one of several possible dictionaries. To make use of this program texts need to be in computer-readable form, but there are now thousands of such texts on the web—out of copyright classics at project gutenberg (http://www.gutenberg.org/catalog/), and newspapers at the internet public library. Such support effectively individualises intensive reading, allowing learners to seek help of various kinds where it is needed in a speedy way that does not take the learners too far away from the text.

There is now a growing body of research supporting the use of concordances, electronic dictionary look-up and hypertext glossing (Cobb, Greaves and Horst, 2001; Cobb, 1997) as aids to vocabulary learning and reading.

## Elaboration

**Elaboration** involves the rewriting of texts but it involves adding to the original text rather than removing or replacing what is there. The unknown words in the text are, in effect, glossed in the text itself. Here is an example of a piece of elaborated text from the novel *Lord Jim.* I have put the elaborations in italics and the words outside the 2,000 word level in bold, but in the text they would not be marked in any way. Note that *apparelled* is not elaborated as the text provides enough elaboration for this word.

He was an inch, perhaps two, under six feet, powerfully built, and he advanced straight at you with a slight **stoop** *or bend* of the shoulders, head forward, and a fixed from-under stare which made you think of a charging *animal like a* **bull**. His voice was deep, loud, and his manner displayed a kind of **dogged** self-**assertion**, *that is always saying things in* *a strong way*, which had nothing **aggressive** *(like attacking someone)* in it. It seemed a **necessity**, *that is, it was something he needed*, and it was directed apparently as much at himself as at anybody else. He was spotlessly neat, **apparelled** in *beautifully* **immaculate** white from shoes to *the* **hat** *on his head*, and in the various eastern ports where he got his living as ship-**chandler**'s water-**clerk** he was very popular. *A ship-chandler provides supplies for ships, and a clerk works for the chandler.*

Although there are no published elaborated texts available, there have been several pieces of research looking at the effect of this elaboration (Chung, 1995; Parker and Chaudron, 1987; Yano, Long and Ross, 1994; Kim, 2006). In general, this research shows that elaborated text seems to work about as well as simplified text.

## The Extensive Reading Programme

This discussion of guidelines for an extensive reading programme has focused mainly on learning conditions and research and has not given attention to more practical factors such as how to organise and manage a library of graded readers, how to obtain graded readers, and how many are needed to set up a library. These issues are well covered in Day and Bamford (1998). The main purpose of this chapter is to convince teachers that it is worthwhile setting up an extensive reading programme, making it a substantial, obligatory part of a course, and persisting with it in an organised way. The results of such programmes (Elley, 1991; Waring and Takaki, 2003) are impressive.

*Note*

This chapter is a revised and updated version of an article entitled "Planning and running an extensive reading programme" published in *NUCB Journal of Language Culture and Communication* 3, 1, 2001, pp 1–8. It is reprinted here with the editor's permission.

# CHAPTER 5

# Reading Faster

In a typical speed reading course, each lesson is like this. The learners each select the text they want to read. The teacher then says, Are you ready? Go!

At this command, 18 heads dip down and the learners begin reading in earnest. At the same time the teacher is pointing to minutes and seconds written on the board, indicating how much time has passed since the learners began reading.

| Minutes | Seconds |
|---------|---------|
| 0       | 00      |
| 1       | 10      |
| 2       | 20      |
| 3       | 30      |
| 4       | 40      |
| 5       | 50      |

As each learner finishes reading the short text (usually around 500–600 words long), they look up at the board, note down the time it took them to read, and then turn over the text and start answering the ten comprehension questions on the back of the sheet. When they have answered the questions, they get their answer key and mark their own answers. They look at the conversion chart and convert their time into words per minute. They enter their speed in words per minute onto the speed graph and they enter their comprehension score out of ten onto the comprehension graph. The teacher moves around the class looking at graphs and giving comments and encouragement to the learners. The whole activity has taken about seven minutes. The same activity will happen two or three times more in the same week and will continue for a total of around seven weeks until most of the 25 texts have been read. This is one lesson in a speed reading course for non-native speakers of English. This chapter looks at the reasons for having such a course. It then examines a range of ways in which reading speed can be increased and maintained.

## The Nature and Limits of Reading Speed

To see what reading speed goals it is sensible to aim for, we need to understand the physical nature of reading and how this relates to reading speed. There are many misconceptions about reading faster, particularly about how fast people can read, and these can be cleared up by looking at the physical nature of reading. When people read, three types of action are involved—fixations on particular words, jumps (saccades) to the next item to focus on, and regressions (movements back to an item already looked at). This means that while reading the eyes do not move smoothly along a line of print, but jump from one word to another. There has been a great deal of research on eye movements while reading and recent improvements in eye-tracking technology have confirmed the following findings (Rayner, 1998).

1. A skilled reader reading at around 250–300 words per minute makes around 90 fixations per 100 words. Most words are fixated on, but function words like *the* and *of* are fixated on much less often than content words. The longer the word, the more likely it is to receive a fixation. If a word is really long, it may receive two or even three fixations. Around 200 milliseconds are spent on each fixation (about five per second). The length of these fixations varies a lot depending on how difficult a word or sentence is to read.
2. Each saccadic jump is around 1.2 words in English. This is about eight letters. In Finnish, where words are longer, the average jump is ten letters. This is around the maximum number of letters that can be seen clearly in one fixation. During the jump no items can be focused on because the eyes are moving. A jump takes about 20 milliseconds. The basic unit in the jump is the word and languages with quite different writing systems (for example, English and Chinese) all tend to have an average of one jump for every 1.2 words.
3. A skilled reader makes around 15 regressions in every 100 fixations. Regressions occur because the reader made too big a jump (many regressions when reading in English are only a few letters long), and because there were problems in understanding the text.

What this research shows is that in normal skilled reading, most words are focused on. As there are limits on the minimum time needed to focus on a word and on the size and speed of a jump, it is possible to calculate the physiological limit on reading speed where reading involves fixating on most of the words in the text. This is around 300 words per minute. (Five fixations per second times 1.2 = 6 words per second times 60 = 360 words per minute. If regressions are considered, this reduces the forward movement through the text to around 300 wpm.) If someone is reading at a speed of 400 words per minute or more, then that person is no longer fixating on most of the words in the text. In Urquhart and Weir's (1998) terms, that person is no longer doing careful reading, but instead is doing "expeditious reading" which includes skimming and scanning. Unless such readers bring a great deal of background knowledge to their reading, they will usually be unable to answer detailed questions on parts of the text not fixated on.

Many non-native speakers of English and some native speakers read at speeds which are well below 300 wpm. About one-quarter of the time in a well-balanced language course should be spent on the strand of fluency development helping learners become more fluent in using the language they already know; that is, making the best use of what they have already learned. This fluency development needs to cover the four skills of listening, speaking, reading and writing and needs to involve substantial amounts of input and output.

The physical symptoms of slow reading are: (1) fixating on units smaller than a word (word parts, letters, parts of letters), thus making several fixations per word; (2) spending a long time on each fixation or on some fixations; and (3) making many regressions to look back at what has already been read. Increasing speed will result in a change in these symptoms.

Reading speed is affected by a range of factors including the purpose of the reading, and the difficulty of the text. The difficulty of the text is affected by the vocabulary, grammatical constructions, discourse, and background knowledge. A reasonable goal for second language learners who are reading material that contains no unknown vocabulary or grammar and that has easy content is around 250 words per minute.

Chung and Nation (2006) looked at the effect of a speed reading course on Korean learners of English at university level. The learners read 23 passages over nine weeks. The passages were all within the first 1,000 words of English (Quinn, Nation and Millett, 2007). Using a very conservative scoring system (the average speed in words per minute of the last three passages read minus the average speed of the first three passages read), the learners began with the speed of 141 wpm and after 20 passages reached on average 214 wpm—an increase in speed of 52 percent. Of the 40 learners, two made no increase. The majority of the learners (30 out of 40) made gradual increases, while four increased erratically with rises and drops, two reached plateaus and stayed there for a while before making further increases, and two had a mixed pattern. Most of the gains were made in the first ten texts, but 11 students out of 40 made most gains in the second ten texts, and most students made some gains in the second ten texts. It is thus worth persisting with speed reading. Hunt and Beglar (unpublished paper) looked at the effect of extensive reading over several months on reading speed and found increases especially for those learners who read simplified texts. The gains of speed were significant but not enormous and may have been greater if learners had followed a focused speed reading course.

## The Nature of Fluency Development

We have looked briefly at the physical aspects of reading and how these change as fluency develops. However, these signs are the result of mental processes. One of the mental processes involved in reading is decoding; that is, turning the written form of a word into a familiar spoken form with a known meaning. Readers develop skill in decoding in two related ways. Through practice they become faster at recognising the unit they are working with and, second, they change the size of this basic unit. When someone begins to read an unfamiliar written script there are many things to notice. Say, for example, an Arabic speaker is learning to read English. Because Arabic uses a different script from English, learning to read the English letters *p b d g* is quite difficult because although the letters have some similarities, there are important differences. Where is the circle part of the letter, at the top or at the bottom, on the left of the stalk or on the right? *p b d* have straight stalks, *g* has a bent stalk. At a very early stage of reading English, each part of a letter is an important piece of information. With practice, fluency in recognising the different letters develops and soon the basic unit that the reader is working with is no longer the parts of the letters but the letters themselves. With further reading experience the basic unit will change from letters to word parts and words. At early stages of word recognition, learners may rely on only some of the letters, usually the initial letters, for word recognition. As they become more accomplished readers, they may no longer need to notice each letter but can recognise whole words and, if necessary, apply rules or use analogy to quickly decode unfamiliar words. What this means is that fluency development involves not just becoming faster, it also involves changing the size and nature of the basic unit that the reader is working with. Another way of putting this is to say that fluency develops when complex activities like reading are made less complex by the fluent mastery of some of the subskills involved in the activity.

Research on speaking fluency (Nation, 1989) provides evidence for this. The **4/3/2** speaking activity involves learners working in pairs and one member of the pair speaking on a familiar topic to the other (the listener) for four minutes. Then they change partners. The speaker remains as a speaker and the listener stays as a listener. The speaker now has to give the same talk to the new partner in three minutes. The partners change again and the same talk is given for two minutes. When the two-minute and four-minute talks are compared, it is typically found that: (1) the speed of speaking has increased in terms of words per minute; (2) the number of hesitations has decreased per 100 words; (3) the number of grammatical errors in repeated sections of the talk has decreased; and (4) there are two or three more complex sentences in the two-minute talk compared with the four-minute talk. For example, if in the four-minute talk the speaker said "We went to Paraparaumu. Paraparaumu is outside Wellington", in the two-minute talk they may say "We went to Paraparaumu which is outside Wellington". Two simple sentences become one complex sentence. Fluency is thus accompanied by improvements in accuracy and complexity (Schmidt, 1992). This is because as parts of the task become more under the control of the speaker, other parts of the task can receive better attention.

There are two main paths to fluency. One could be called "the well-beaten path" and the 4/3/2 activity is an example of this. In such activities, repetition of the same material is used to develop fluency. By doing something over and over again you get better at doing it. The second path to fluency could be called "the rich and varied map". In such activities, the learners do things which differ slightly from each other but which draw on the same kind of knowledge. A good example of this is easy extensive reading where learners read lots of graded readers at the same level. The stories differ but the same vocabulary and grammatical constructions reoccur and the learners develop a rich range of associations with the words and constructions.

## The Nature of Fluency Development Activities

If an activity is going to contribute effectively to fluency development, then it needs to meet certain conditions. Let us look at a very useful fluency development activity for reading aloud to see what these conditions are.

**Repeated reading** has been used with good results with first language readers to help reach a good degree of oral reading fluency (Samuels, 1979;

Dowhower, 1989; Rasinski, 1990; Sindelar, Monda and O'Shea, 1990). The learner reads a text (about 50–300 words long) aloud, with help where necessary, while the teacher or another learner listens. Then the text is re-read reasonably soon after (within a day). Then the text is read again a day later. The text should only be a little bit above the learner's present level. Most of the running words should easily be recognised. The optimal number of repetitions is around three to five. Using texts intended to be read aloud, like poems, plays, jokes or stories can increase the purposefulness of the activity. Repeated reading and repeated reading while listening to a taped passage give similar positive results.

The first condition needed for a fluency development activity is that the learners should be focused on the message. In repeated reading this condition is met by having a listener. The reader is trying to communicate the message of the text to the listener. The second condition needed is that the material should be easy. It is important to choose texts for repeated reading where all the vocabulary is known and there are not too many irregularly spelt words. The third condition for a fluency activity is that there should be some pressure to perform at a faster than normal speed. In the repeated reading activity the repetition provides this encouragement. To strengthen this condition, the time taken to read the text could be noted for each reading and the reader should be trying to beat their previous speed for the same text. The fourth and final condition is that there should be quantity of practice. In repeated reading, the text is not very long but the repetitions mean that there is quite a lot of reading practice. To truly be a fluency development activity these four conditions need to be met.

Let us now look at a range of reading activities that meet these conditions and that are thus very useful for developing reading fluency. The activities are divided into three groups which are in order of development. The first group of reading fluency activities involve reading aloud. Such reading is a very important first step towards the second group of activities which involve careful silent reading. The third group involve "expeditious reading" or skimming and scanning very quickly to get a particular piece or a particular type of information. Skill in careful silent reading is an important prerequisite to most skimming and scanning.

### Increasing Oral Reading Speed

**Reading aloud** has not been looked on very favourably in the second language reading class, mainly because of the misuse of the technique of reading aloud around the class. However, in the first language classroom, reading aloud to the teacher or to a peer is a very important step towards gaining fluent decoding and comprehending skills which are a necessary preparation for fluent silent reading. There are several useful activities for working on oral reading and they have just as much value in the second language class as in the first. What all these activities have in common is a learner reading aloud, trying to convey the message of the text to a sympathetic and interested listener. In small classes this may involve a learner reading to the teacher, but in most classes it will involve pair work where a learner reads to a classmate.

We have already looked at **repeated reading**. A strength of this technique is that it can be used with material that has some difficulties for the reader. By repetition these difficulties are overcome and in the later repetitions the activity can thus meet the conditions needed for fluency development.

**Paired reading** is a form of assisted reading. In this activity, the learner is paired with a more proficient reader. They sit side by side and read the same text aloud together with the more proficient reader keeping at the same speed as the less proficient reader. The less proficient reader nudges the more proficient reader as a signal that they want to read alone. If the less proficient reader strikes problems, the more proficient reader joins in reading again. Word recognition errors are corrected as soon as they happen, simply by the proficient reader saying the word without further explanation. The same activity can be used with a parent or an older or more proficient learner. A paired reading activity can last for about 15 to 30 minutes, and the learners should be trained in the use of the procedure. Research on this activity with first language learners shows that learners make very substantial progress in accuracy and comprehension. The tutors also make progress in their reading (Rasinski and Hoffman, 2003; Topping, 1989).

**4/3/2 reading** is an adaptation of the 4/3/2 speaking activity (Nation, 1989) for reading aloud. Each learner has a text to read. All the learners could have the same text but it is more interesting for the listeners and more suitable for a class with a wide range of proficiency if they all have different texts. The learners form pairs. One member of each pair is the listener and the other is the reader. When the teacher says "Go!" each reader reads their text to their listener. After four minutes the teacher says "Stop!" and the readers stop reading. They change partners and the readers then read the same text for three minutes to their new listener. They change partners again and the readers now read the same text to the new listener for two minutes. The learners are told that they should try to speed up each reading so that each listener hears about the same amount of text even though the time is less. As a variation, after each reading the reader can mark in pencil the place in the text they reached.

A part of the class time can be set aside for **extensive reading aloud** where learners read to each other or where one learner reads a continuing story to a small group. The story should be easy to read and the reader can concentrate on making it interesting. A variation could be learners making a tape-recording of a story for others to listen to.

The **read-and-look-up** activity does not meet many of the conditions for a fluency activity but it is one that encourages learners to work with a larger basic unit. Michael West (1960: 12–13) devised this technique as a way of helping learners to learn from written dialogues and to help them put expression into the dialogues. West regarded the physical aspects of read-and-look-up as being very important for using the technique properly. The learners work in pairs facing each other. One is the reader, the other is the listener. The reader holds the piece of paper or the book containing the dialogue at about chest level and slightly to the left. This enables the reader to look at the piece of paper and then to look at the listener, moving only their eyes and not having to move their head at all. The reader looks at the piece of paper and tries to remember as long a phrase as possible. The reader can look at the paper for as long as is necessary. Then, when ready, they look at the listener and say the phrase. While they look at the paper, they do not speak. While they speak they do not look at the paper. These rules force the reader to rely on memory. At first the technique is a little difficult to use because the reader has to discover what length of phrase is most comfortable and has to master the rules of the technique. It can also be practised at home in front of a mirror. West saw value in the technique because the learner "has to carry the words of a whole phrase, or perhaps a whole sentence, in his mind. The connection is not from book to mouth, but from book to brain, and then from brain to mouth. That interval of memory constitutes half the learning process . . . Of all methods of learning a language, Read-and-Look-up is, in our opinion, the most valuable" (West, 1960: 12).

Good spoken reading speeds range from 100 to 200 words per minute. These are necessarily slower speeds than silent reading speeds.

Reading aloud is a useful activity to practise accurate decoding and it is a useful activity in its own right—people gain pleasure from listening to stories and talks and from reading stories to others. The activities in this section provide a useful preparation for the silent reading activities described in the next section.

### Increasing Careful Silent Reading Speed

The classic way of increasing reading speed is to follow a **speed reading course** consisting of timed readings followed by comprehension measures. For learners of English as a second or foreign language, such courses need to be within a controlled vocabulary so that the learners are not held up by unknown words. The first published course for foreign learners of English was *Reading Faster* by Edward Fry (1967) which had an accompanying teachers' book called *Teaching Faster Reading* (Fry 1965). The course consisted of texts around 500 words long, each followed by ten multiple-choice questions. The texts were taken from a graded reader and were written at the 2,000 word level. The course worked well but it was not suitable for learners with vocabularies of less than 2,000 words and it also contained the names of diseases like *kwashiorkor* and *yaws* which tended to slow the reading. Quinn and Nation (1974) developed a course written well within the first 1,000 words of English consisting of 25 texts, each exactly 550 words long, and followed by ten comprehension questions. Millett (Quinn, Nation and Millett, 2007) has revised the Quinn and Nation text and has produced two other texts, one at the 2,000 word level and one at the 2,000 plus Academic Word List level (Millett, 2005) (see also Nation and Malarcher, 2007). Other speed reading courses have not used a controlled vocabulary and this has meant that they do not meet the conditions needed for fluency development.

There have been mechanical reading pacers where the text is revealed at a pre-set speed and there have been films which reveal text at a certain rate. Such aids are fun but are not necessary for increasing reading speed. The essential requirements are suitable texts and questions.

**Easy extensive reading** is another very effective way of increasing reading speed by asking learners to read graded readers at a level which is much easier than the level they would normally read to gain meaning-focused input. Learners should be encouraged to do large quantities of such reading and to re-read books that they have really enjoyed. It is important to remember that there need to be two types of extensive reading involving graded readers. One type, reading for meaning-focused input, involves learners reading at a level where about one word in 50 is unknown. These words can be guessed from context and add to the readers' vocabulary knowledge. The second type of extensive reading, reading for fluency development, should involve texts where there are virtually no unknown words. Such texts should be read quickly for enjoyment, and large numbers of them should be read.

In **silent repeated reading**, the learners silently re-read texts that they have read before. In order to encourage faster reading, they can note the time each reading took so that they have the goal of reading it faster each time.

**Issue logs** are a very effective way of involving learners. At the beginning of a language course the learners each decide on a topic that they will research each week. Each learner should have a different topic. The topics can include pollution, global warming, oil, traffic accidents, the stock market, etc. Each week the learners find newspaper reports, magazine articles, academic texts, information from the internet, television reports, and so on, on their topic and write a brief summary. As they are reading lots of material on the same topic, they will soon be in control of the relevant vocabulary and will bring a lot of background knowledge to what they read (Watson, 2004).

Careful silent reading is the most common kind of reading. Learners need to be able to read with good comprehension near the upper speed limits of such reading.

## Increasing Silent Expeditious Reading Speed

There are two major kinds of expeditious reading—**skimming** and **scanning**. The major goal of expeditious reading would be to increase skimming speed. In skimming the reader goes through a text quickly, not noting every word but trying to get the main idea of what the text is about. This is sometimes called getting the gist of the text. After such reading the reader is unlikely to have noticed details, but should be able to say in a general way what the text is about. The more background knowledge that a reader brings to skimming, the faster the skimming speed is likely to be. Reading speeds higher than 300–400 words per minute are the result of skimming, not careful reading.

Being able to skim text is a useful skill because skimming can be used to help decide if a text or section of a text deserves careful reading. Skimming activities should involve texts which are at least 2,000 words long and which are on topics that the learners are familiar with. Comprehension should be measured by questions which ask "What was the text about?". Multiple-choice or true/false questions which focus on the gist of the text could also be used.

**Scanning** involves searching for a particular piece of information in a text, such as looking for a particular name or a particular number. It is probably better to spend time increasing skimming speed than to devise scanning activities. This is because effective scanning depends on good careful reading and skimming skills, and training in scanning is unlikely to result in more fluent access to items. This is worth researching.

Typical scanning tasks include searching a text for a particular quotation, someone's name, a particular date or number, or a particular word; or searching a list for a telephone number, someone's name, or a particular word or phrase.

**Frequently Asked Questions About Reading Speed**

*What About Comprehension?*

Comprehension is very important when developing fluency in reading. There is no point in reading faster if little is understood. For careful silent reading, readers should score seven or eight out of ten on a comprehension test. Higher scores than this indicate that the reader is going too slowly and is trying to get too much from the text. It would be easy for the reader to increase their speed. Scores of six or less out of ten are too low and the reader should read subsequent texts at the same speed until comprehension improves. Speed reading courses use both words per minute graphs and comprehension score graphs. Lower comprehension scores are acceptable for skimming tasks, because while skimming readers do not give attention to every part of the text. Questions on skimming texts should look for the main ideas.

*How can Reading Fluency be Measured?*

The typical measure for all kinds of fluency tasks is words per minute (see Lennon (1990) for a wide range of measures for speaking fluency). There has been some debate over whether syllables per minute is a more precise measure, but the difficulty in counting syllables is much greater than any small returns in accuracy it may bring. Moreover, research into eye movements suggests that words not syllables are the primary unit of attention. A useful compromise when doing research may be to use standard word units, that is counting the number of letters in the text (easily done by a word processor) and dividing by eight. Carver (1982) has used six character spaces as the standard word measure, but the speed reading research suggests that eight character spaces may be a more justifiable measure.

*How can Progress in Reading Fluency be Monitored?*

- *One minute reading.* An interesting activity for regularly checking on reading speed is one minute reading (Iwano, 2004). The learners read a text with the time being recorded by a stopwatch. After exactly one minute the teacher says "Stop!", and the learners mark where they reached in the text. They count how many words there are up to that point. Doing this on the same text before and after a speed reading programme can be a good way of showing learners how their speed has increased.
- *Reading logs.* A log is a regular record of what happened at particular times. Learners can keep a log of their extensive reading, noting the name of the book, the time they started reading and how much they

read. If this is accurately done, it may provide a rough indicator of reading speed and increases in speed.

- *Speed reading graphs.* When learners do a speed reading course with short texts and questions, they score their speed and comprehension on graphs (see Quinn, Nation and Millett, 2007). Teachers should regularly look at learners' graphs and give them advice and encouragement. Where progress is not being made, the teacher can suggest remedial procedures like repeated reading, skimming before reading, and discussion and prediction of the content with a friend before reading.

### What are Good Reading Speeds?

A good oral reading speed is around 150 words per minute. A good careful silent reading speed is around 250 words per minute. A good skimming speed is around 500 words per minute. These are reasonable goals for foreign and second language learners who are reading material that contains no unknown vocabulary and grammar.

### What are the Advantages and Disadvantages of Reading Faster?

There are disadvantages of reading faster. The pressure to go faster can be a source of stress. Such pressure can reduce the enjoyment that learners get from reading. It is best to see the skill of reading faster as providing a wider range of choices for a reader. Sometimes it is good to read fast. At other times it is not. Being able to make the choice is an advantage.

Research on reading faster has shown that increasing reading speed in one language can result in increases in another known language. This has been tested from the first language to English (Bismoko and Nation, 1974) and from English to the first language (Cramer, 1975; West, 1941). It is likely that the transfer of training here is the transfer of confidence; that is, the confidence that you can read faster and still comprehend.

It has been suggested that reading too slowly at speeds of much less than 100 words per minute can have negative effects on comprehension. Anyone who has learned to read another script knows the phenomenon of slowly sounding out the script and then having to go back and read the sentence again more fluently to see what it means.

Fluency development is an essential strand in a language course (for a discussion of listening and speaking fluency, see the companion book in this series (Nation and Newton, 2009), *Teaching ESL/EFL Listening and Speaking*. Learners need to be able to make the best use of what they already know at every stage of their learning. Giving attention to reading fluency is one part of this strand. As with the development of listening fluency, speaking fluency and writing fluency, the development of reading fluency can have clear practical and motivational benefits for a language learner.

*Note*

I am grateful to Jukka Hyona of the University of Turku in Finland for comments on a part of this chapter.

CHAPTER **6**

# Assessing Reading

There are several reasons for assessing reading and the skills and knowledge that are involved in reading. They include assessing to encourage learning, assessing to monitor progress and provide feedback, assessing to diagnose problems, and assessing to measure proficiency. The same form of assessment may be used for a variety of goals. Table 6.1 lists these reasons and their applications, and they are expanded on in the rest of the chapter.

Good assessment needs to be reliable, valid and practical. Reliability is helped by having a high number of points of measurement, by using a test format that the learners are familiar with, and by using consistent delivery and marking procedures. Validity is helped by using reliable measures, and by being clear about what is being measured and why. The practicality of a test can be helped by giving very careful thought to how the learners will answer the test and how it will be marked. The ease of making a test is also part of its practicality.

## Motivating

A very common use of informal assessment is to make learners study. At the worst they study because there will be a test, but preferably success in the test maintains their interest in study. Regular comprehension tests can do this, but there are other ways as well which do not involve formal testing.

**Table 6.1** Goals, Purposes and Means of Reading Assessment

| Goals of assessment | Purposes | Ways of assessing |
|---|---|---|
| Motivate | Encourage learning | Reading logs<br>Book reports<br>Comprehension tests<br>Speed reading graphs |
| Measure achievement | Monitor progress<br>Guide teaching<br>Provide feedback to the learner<br>Award a grade | Comprehension tests<br>Speed reading graphs |
| Diagnose problems | Isolate reading difficulties<br>Provide focused help | Reading aloud<br>Vocabulary tests<br>Receptive grammar tests<br>Translation<br>Speed reading tests |
| Measure proficiency | Award a grade<br>See if standards are achieved | Comprehension tests<br>Cloze tests<br>Speed reading tests |

*Speed Reading Graphs*

When learners do a regular speed reading course they keep a graph of their speed and a graph of their comprehension, and for each passage they read, the results are entered on the graphs. This can be highly motivating for learners, particularly if their speed can be seen to increase and their comprehension remains steady. Similar graphs for comprehension are used with the SRA reading boxes. These graphs can be even more motivating if a goal is set. For speed reading this could be a goal of around 300 words per minute.

*Reading Logs*

A log is a regular record of work done. When learners do extensive reading, they can keep a log noting the title, level, degree of enjoyment, and time taken to read for each graded reader or other book they read. Bamford and Day (2004) have several suggestions about the form of these logs.

*Oral Book Reports*

Oral book reports involve learners talking to the class or a group of learners about a book they have just read. The goal of the report should not be to describe the book in detail but to make others interested in reading it without giving away the ending or exciting parts.

The use of assessment as a motivator has the aim of getting the learners to read so that eventually they will not need assessment to motivate them.

## Measuring Achievement

Measures of achievement focus on the learning done in a particular course. If a course has focused on speed reading, then the achievement measure would be a speed reading measure even though speed of reading is only a part of the larger picture of reading proficiency. Similarly, if the course has focused on reading academic texts, the achievement measure could be a comprehension measure using academic texts. Achievement measures are thus closely related to the course of which they are part. They need to have a high level of face validity; that is, they should clearly look like what they are supposed to be measuring. Since reading comprehension is a common goal of reading courses we will focus on that in this section. Achievement tests, however, could test various reading strategies, speed of reading, word recognition, reading aloud, or note-taking from reading, depending on the goals of the course.

Comprehension tests can use a variety of question forms and can have a variety of focuses. Here we will look at the various forms and consider their reliability, validity, and practicality.

### Pronominal Questions, Imperatives

These questions require learners to make a written answer which can range in length from a single word to several paragraphs. Usually for comprehension, short answers are required and these forms of questions are called short answer questions. If the answers the learners have to make are short, then more questions can be answered, thus increasing the reliability and validity of the test. These questions can be used for all focuses of comprehension. They are suited to checking literal comprehension because it is not difficult to write the questions avoiding the same words that are used in the reading text. They are suited to inferences, application and responding critically because the learners have to search for and construct their own answers using what is found in the text. Another positive feature of these types of questions is that they can be marked using a grading scale, for example 0, ½, 1 or 0, 1, 2, 3 marks for each question depending on the completeness and accuracy of the answer. This allows credit to be given for partial comprehension and credit to be given for high quality comprehension.

These positive features have their corresponding disadvantages. When learners write their own answers, a range of differently worded answers is likely to occur. Markers then have to be consistent and fair in the way they score these answers. This is primarily an issue of reliability. It is best dealt with by making and adding to a list of possible answers with their corresponding marks, and getting another teacher or highly proficient reader to answer the test and then afterwards to check the list of possible answers.

This prechecking by another teacher may result in changes to the questions to limit the answers that are possible. The answer sheet where the learners write their answers can have a set space for each answer and learners have to keep their answers within the limits of that space.

*True/False, Yes/No, Alternative Questions and Multiple-choice*

These question forms are all grouped together because the answer to the question is contained within the question or instructions, and thus the learners do not have to compose their answer. This simplifies marking. In the following discussion we will focus on multiple-choice questions because these are the most difficult to make. Typically there is a stem with four choices, one of which is correct. In order to produce a large number of questions to make the test reliable, quite a long text or several short texts are needed. Marking is usually very easy, and most learners are familiar with multiple-choice tests, although they may not have good strategies for sitting them. Good multiple-choice tests tend to be very reliable.

Multiple-choice questions can focus on details (microstructure) and on more general aspects (macrostructure) of the text, although some researchers have found difficulty in using multiple-choice to measure global comprehension. Multiple-choice tests only involve reading and so the measurement is less likely to be affected by writing skill than it is in a short answer test. If a multiple-choice test has not been well prepared, learners may be able to get a reasonable score without reading the text, and part of the preparation of a good test involves checking this. Multiple-choice questions can be checked by checking the length of the answers to make sure that the correct answer is not always shorter or longer than the distractors, asking a native speaker to answer the test to see if they get all of the answers correct, getting a colleague to look critically at the items to see if they can see any problems with them, and looking at learners' answers to the items to see if some items are too easy or too hard or if the learners are all choosing the same wrong choice.

To make marking easier, a special answer sheet and an answer key may be used. Learners circle the correct answer. Because of the ease of marking, multiple-choice is useful when there are very large numbers of tests to mark. Computer marking is possible. Practicality is a strength of using multiple-choice tests. However, making multiple-choice tests is not easy. Making four plausible choices is usually a challenge and good multiple-choice questions require a lot of trialling.

*Information Transfer*

Incomplete information transfer diagrams can be used to measure comprehension of a text. See Figure 6.1 later in this chapter for an example.

The learners read the text and fill in the diagram with short notes. The advantages are that the information the learner produces can cover a lot of points and yet need not involve a lot of writing. The disadvantage is in gaining consistency in marking.

## Diagnosing Problems

If a learner is having problems with reading, it is very useful to be able to see where the problems lie. As reading is a complex skill, there are many possible sources of difficulty. So if a learner performs badly on a proficiency measure such as a cloze test or a comprehension test, it is useful to have a procedure which can be followed to find the reasons for the poor performance.

There are four general principles that should be followed. First, diagnosing problems should be done on an individual basis. That is, diagnostic testing should be done with the teacher sitting next to the individual learner and carefully observing what happens. There are several reasons for this. If testing is done with the whole class, individual learners may not give their best effort. In addition, a teacher needs to be able to observe what aspects of the diagnostic task are causing difficulty, and should be able to adjust the testing procedure during the process to get the best information about an individual's problems. Second, diagnosing problems should begin with the smallest units involved and go step by step to the larger units. From a reading perspective, this means starting with word identification, moving to vocabulary knowledge, then to comprehension of single sentences, and then to text comprehension and reading speed. The assumption behind this progression is that the various smaller units combine to contribute to the larger units. Third, as much as possible, learners should feel comfortable with and relaxed during diagnostic testing. This is a difficult principle to apply because in such testing it is obvious to the learner that they are being evaluated in some way. The principle, however, can be applied by the teacher beginning with very easy tasks where the learner can be successful, giving praise for effort and success, being friendly, and frequently taking small breaks to help the learner relax. Fourth, do not rely on only one test. Even where it seems obvious where the problem lies, use a different kind of test possibly at a different level of unit size to double check. Decisions about a learner's level of skill can have far-reaching effects on their learning. It is worth spending time to get the best possible information.

### Reading Aloud

Reading aloud can be used to check the learner's skill at word recognition. As a very cautious first step it is worth observing carefully to see if the learner's eyesight is good. This could be done by getting them to look at a picture and then asking them questions about it. Quite a large proportion of males are colour-blind to some degree, but that should not affect reading. If the learner seems to have eyesight problems, it is worth getting their eyesight tested by a specialist.

Reading aloud should begin with a very easy short text. If the learner has problems in reading aloud very early in the text, it may be worthwhile pausing and talking about the context of the story with the learner, discussing some of the ideas that will occur in the text and predicting what might happen in the story. It is probably not worth keeping a running record of errors for the first text, but if it becomes clear that word recognition is a major problem, then keeping such a record would be useful. If the learner has some problems with word recognition these could be checked against the correspondences in Appendix 1 to see if they are irregular items or if there is some pattern to the errors.

A difficulty with reading aloud for second language learners is that their skill in reading may be greater than their skill in speaking and so their spoken production may be a poor representation of their reading. Talking to the learner before the reading begins is one way of checking this.

*Vocabulary Tests*

Learners may have difficulty reading because they do not know enough vocabulary. Note that word recognition during reading aloud is affected by vocabulary knowledge and so very easy texts need to be used at first when testing reading aloud. Similarly, if the vocabulary test is a written test which requires the learners to read the test items, then the measure of vocabulary knowledge will be affected by word recognition skills. Learners may have a large spoken vocabulary but be unable to read the words they know.

The following vocabulary tests can be used with learners of English.

The Bilingual Levels Tests

Here is an item from the Indonesian version of the test (available in Nation, 2004b).

```
1 could
2 during        ____dapat, bisa
3 this          ____selama
4 piece         ____supaya
5 of
6 in order to
```

These are tests of the first and second 1,000 words of West's (1953) *General Service List*. They are available in the following languages—Japanese,

Indonesian, Thai, Korean, Chinese (traditional and simplified), Tagalog, Samoan, Tongan, Russian, and Vietnamese. The test is easily marked with a marking key. Each of the two levels has 30 items, which is enough for a good level of reliability. The validity of the test is strengthened for low-proficiency learners by the use of the first language to represent the meanings of the words. The learners do not have to deal with the more complex language of English definitions. The words are tested out of context and this can cause problems for words that can have different meanings, such as *seal* which can mean "to close tightly" or "the marine mammal", or *bear* which can mean "to carry" or "to put up with". The teacher should sit next to the learner while the test is being done to make sure that the learner takes the test seriously, follows a sensible test-taking strategy, knows how to handle the slightly unusual test format, and is not experiencing reading problems which might interfere with the sitting of the test. It is very important that the teacher does this because it has happened that a whole class of learners sitting a test have not taken it seriously and have got low marks. In this case, the teacher then set up a programme to teach the vocabulary which the learners actually already knew.

The True/False Vocabulary Test

Here are three sample items (available in Nation, 2001: 412–415; Nation, 2004b; Nation, 1993).

> When something falls, it goes up.
> Most children go to school at night.
> It is easy for children to remain still.

There are two versions of this 40-item test of the first 1,000 words of West's (1953) *General Service List.* The test can be given in a written form or, if necessary, it can be given orally. There are enough items to get a good level of reliability. The words are tested in sentences and learners need to understand the sentence and apply it to their knowledge of the world in order to make a decision about whether the sentence is true or false. As there are factors other than vocabulary knowledge involved in the test, this affects the validity of the test. Whether this effect is positive or negative depends on what you want to test, words alone or words in use.

Other possible tests include the yes/no test, and the monolingual levels test (Schmitt, Schmitt and Clapham, 2001).

*Tests of Grammatical Knowledge*

If the teacher speaks the first language of the learners, the most straightforward test of grammatical knowledge is to get the learners to translate sentences from reading texts, starting with a very simple text. A validity issue with this is that such translation may encourage word by word reading and as a result mistranslation. This can be discouraged by asking the learner to read the whole sentence first before beginning the translation. An example of mistranslation is "He made the theory useful" being translated as "He made the theory which was useful".

If the teacher does not speak the learners' first language, sentence completion tests could be used, for example,

I was very surprised by_____.
It made me_____.
I_____waiting for at least an hour.

Note that grammar tests, both translation and completion, involve word recognition skills and vocabulary knowledge as well as grammatical knowledge. It is thus important that the learners' word recognition skills and vocabulary knowledge are tested before grammar knowledge is tested.

### Testing Reading Speed

If learners read very slowly, their comprehension can be affected, either because they do not have enough time to complete the reading or because their reading is so slow that ideas within and between sentences are not properly integrated.

If reading speed is thought to be a problem, the speed of reading aloud should be checked first. When doing this, it must be remembered that for a native speaker speaking speed is slower than reading speed. So, a spoken reading speed of around 100 to 150 words per minute is fast.

If the speed of reading aloud seems fast enough, the speed of silent reading should be measured. This should be done more than once, preferably three times, in order to get a reliable measure of speed. A speed of more than 100 words per minute is desirable. Untrained native speakers can read at 250 words per minute and this is also a sensible goal for non-native speakers reading easy material. If the silent reading speed is very slow, then the suggestions in Chapter 5 on developing fluent reading need to be followed.

### Other Causes

We have focused on the language aspects of reading in this section on diagnosis. Language issues are only one aspect of reading. Learners may have difficulty in reading for good reasons. They may not want to read. They might not have the necessary background knowledge to read certain texts. They might feel embarrassed to be singled out for attention by the teacher. They might be physically ill or very tired. They may have trouble focusing on a task, or they may have mental problems. The language teacher,

however, must be able to diagnose problems involving language knowledge, but if the problems lie elsewhere, the language teacher may then
need to seek help from others who are more capable of dealing with them.

## Measuring Reading Proficiency

A proficiency test tries to measure a learner's skill not in relation to what
has been taught on a particular course but in relation to a wider standard.
Tests like the TOEFL test and IELTS test are proficiency measures. New
Zealand has reading proficiency tests for school-age native speakers of
English in the Progressive Achievement Tests (PAT) series.

Typically such tests use multiple-choice questions with several texts. In
some tests, cloze tests may be used but these are not so popular, probably for
reasons of face validity rather than because of the effectiveness of the tests.

We have looked at multiple-choice tests in the section on achievement
tests. We will look at cloze tests first in detail in this section.

### Cloze Tests

Here is an example of a cloze test. The complete text is given in Figure 6.1
later in this chapter.

---

***Return Ticket, Please!***
by David Hill

The first person ever to stand on the moon was Neil Armstrong on
20 July 1969.
As he stepped out (1)_____ his spacecraft, he said, "(2)_____'s
one small step (3)_____ a man; one giant (4)_____ for
mankind." What would (5)_____ say if you were (6)_____
first person ever to (7)_____ onto another planet? The
(8)_____ States, working with other (9)_____, is planning a
new (10)_____ to Mars by the (11)_____ 2020. And this
time, (12)_____'ll be people on (13)_____. Spacecraft without crews have (14)_____ landing on Mars since (15)_____
1970s. In 1997, the (16)_____ Pathfinder landed on Mars,
(17)_____ a small, six-wheeled (18)_____ called Sojourner
trundled around, (19)_____ rocks and measuring the
(20)_____ speed. A trip to (21)_____ takes a long time.
(22)_____ astronauts who walked on (23)_____ moon took
three days (24)_____ get there, travelling at (25)_____ km/h
in their Apollo (26)_____. At the same speed, (27)_____

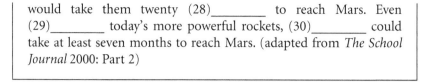

would take them twenty (28)_____ to reach Mars. Even
(29)_____ today's more powerful rockets, (30)_____ could
take at least seven months to reach Mars. (adapted from *The School
Journal* 2000: Part 2)

Every fifth word has been taken out of a reading passage that the learners have never seen before. The learners must fill in the missing words by
guessing. They look at the words before and after the empty space to help
them guess the missing words. The test measures how close the reader's
thought is to the writer's thought.

Usually in a test like this, there need to be 40–50 empty spaces to reach a
good level of reliability. The words must be taken out according to a plan.
Every fifth word can be left out, or every sixth or seventh, etc., but it must
be done in a regular way. A line is drawn to show each missing word.
Usually the first sentence in the text has no words removed. There are two
ways of marking. One way is to accept any sensible answer (acceptable
alternative). Another way is to accept only the words that are exactly the
same as the ones left out (exact replacement). This last way is the easiest for
the teacher and gives the same result. That is, the marks of the learners
will be different when you mark in the two different ways, but the learners
in a class will be ranked in the same order. The cloze test does the same
job as a multiple-choice test and is much easier to make. According to
Anderson (1971) the relationship between the results of a cloze test and
the results of a multiple-choice test on the same passage is as follows. Note
that good scores on the cloze test are 53 percent or above. In exact
replacement marking, learners are not expected to be able to get every item
correct.

| Cloze score | Multiple-choice score | Difficulty of passage |
|---|---|---|
| above 53% | 90% | good for reading alone (independent level) |
| 44%–53% | 75% | good for learning (instructional level) |
| below 44% | below 75% | too difficult (frustration level) |

When marking the test, mis-spellings do not lose marks, but the words
must be grammatically correct. That is, the words should be the correct
part of speech and the correct tense, and should show if they are singular
or plural.

The cloze test makes the learner use the information available in the
passage to predict what the missing parts are. Radice (1978) suggests that
when the cloze exercise is used for teaching, a marking system can be used.

For example, seven marks for the correct answer, six marks for a suitable word of similar meaning, five for a reasonable word with the same meaning, four for the correct content but wrong part of speech, three for the correct part of speech and wrong content, and so on.

A cloze test can be marked very quickly using a test paper with holes in it that fits over the test paper, with the correct answer written above each hole. If every fifth word is deleted two templates need to be used, otherwise there are too many holes. Typically one mark is given for every correct answer. Just under 50 percent of the words in a fixed deletion cloze test are likely to be function words. Most of the focus of the test is on local comprehension. Studies show that less than 10 percent of a cloze test score is dependent on reading across sentence boundaries (Rye, 1985).

The cloze test was originally designed not to measure learners but to measure the readability of texts (Taylor, 1953) and is still used for that purpose (see Brown, 1997).

Brown (1980) tested four ways of scoring the cloze test—exact replacement, acceptable alternative, clozentropy, and multiple-choice. He used a variety of reliability and validity measures as well as assessing practicality. His results showed that all had high validity compared with each other and with a language placement test. All were highly reliable. Considering all criteria, the acceptable alternative was the best, closely followed by exact replacement.

Selective Cloze

A cloze test can be made by leaving out any word that the teacher wants to, instead of every fifth word, etc. This test is more difficult if the empty spaces are not shown. Here is an example.

> The easiest way is always the best way. Often because is difficult to do, we value much more . . .

In this example, one word is missing from each line. The learners must find the place and write the missing word (George, 1972).

> Two old men lived near small town.
> They were friends they were small children. But
> one man bought a car, his friend bought
> one too. He was not if his friend was
> better him.

*Good Comprehension Questions (and how to check if they are good)*

Figure 6.1 consists of a short extract with some accompanying questions. This will be used to provide examples of the features of good comprehension questions described below.

*Return Ticket, Please!*
by David Hill

The first person ever to stand on the moon was Neil Armstrong on 20 July 1969. As he stepped out of his spacecraft, he said, "That's one small step for a man; one giant leap for mankind." What would you say if you were the first person ever to step onto another planet? The United States, working with other countries, is planning a new mission to Mars by the year 2020. And this time, there'll be people on board. Spacecraft without crews have been landing on Mars since the 1970s. In 1997, the spacecraft Pathfinder landed on Mars, and a small, six-wheeled robot called Sojourner trundled around, testing rocks and measuring the wind speed. A trip to Mars takes a long time. The astronauts who walked on the moon took three days to get there, travelling at 6000 km/h in their Apollo spacecraft. At the same speed, it would take them twenty months to reach Mars. Even with today's more powerful rockets, it could take at least seven months to reach Mars.

**Multiple-choice questions**
Draw a circle around the best answer for each question according to the information in the text.

1. What was "a giant leap for mankind"?
   - (a)   sending a spacecraft to the moon
   - (b)   the United States working with other countries
   - (c)   sending a mission to Mars
   - (d)   humans landing on the moon

2. Who have walked on the moon?
   - (a)   no-one
   - (b)   only Neil Armstrong
   - (c)   several people
   - (d)   Sojourner

3. "trundled" (line 9) means
   - (a)   travelled
   - (b)   looked
   - (c)   took many photographs
   - (d)   turned

4. Pathfinder was
   - (a)   a robot
   - (b)   a person

(c)  a spacecraft
(d)  a computer

5. What planet is likely to be the next one for humans to land on?
    (a)  the moon
    (b)  Mars
    (c)  Apollo
    (d)  Venus

6. What did the robot Sojourner do?
    (a)  gather information
    (b)  control the spacecraft Pathfinder
    (c)  explore the moon
    (d)  go with humans to Mars

7. According to the text, a major problem with space travel is
    (a)  the lack of cooperation between countries
    (b)  the cost of robots
    (c)  wind speed
    (d)  the travelling time

8. The 2020 mission to Mars will
    (a)  involve the robot Sojourner
    (b)  take over 40 months of travel
    (c)  be the first time a spacecraft will land on Mars
    (d)  carry humans to the planet

**Information transfer**
Complete each part of the table. Some have been filled for you.

| Year | Spacecraft | Going to | With humans? Yes/No | Travelling time to get there |
|---|---|---|---|---|
| | Apollo | | | |
| | | | | more than 7 months |
| by 2020 | | | | |

**Short answer**
1. Armstrong landed on the moon in the year _____.

2. The 2020 mission to Mars will carry _____.
3. Apollo took _____ days to reach the moon.

**Figure 6.1** Return Ticket, Please!: A Range of Comprehension Test Formats

Good comprehension questions have the following features.

Reliability

- The learners should know how to go about answering the questions. This means that the format of the test should be familiar to the learners and the instructions should be clear. If the test involves making a written answer, the learner should know how long and detailed these answers need to be. If the test is a multiple-choice test, the learner should know how to indicate the right answer and should have had some practice using a strategy to answer multiple-choice questions. To check this, the test and test instructions should be trialled with a few learners of a similar level. A test of similar format could be used with the learners a week or two before to get them used to the format. In the *Return Ticket, Please!* example note that learners are told to draw a circle around the correct answer. "Choose the correct answer" is not precise enough. Note also that they are told to make their choice "according to the information in the text". Most learners are familiar with multiple-choice activities, but it is worth checking with younger learners that they know what to do. Doing the information transfer part of the test could be more confusing. Learners may feel unsure about whether to use phrases or complete sentences, and whether to use their own words or words from the text. Having provided the table already partly filled solves these problems.
- The marking must be fair and consistent. If the same marker remarked the tests, the learners should get the same score. If different people marked the tests, they should give the same score. This is helped if there is an answer key listing the answers with instructions about marking. To check this, get someone else to mark a few tests you have marked. Marking the information transfer part of the test will involve decisions that could affect the consistency of marking. The table in Figure 6.1 has been deliberately made so that the answers are short and can be copied from the text.
- The questions should be easy to understand. This affects both reliability and validity. Comprehending the questions should be easier than comprehending the text. Answering might be difficult, but understanding the questions should not be difficult. If a question is difficult

to understand, then it will not be clear if a wrong answer was the result of poor comprehension of the text or poor comprehension of the question. To check this, check the vocabulary level and grammatical complexity of the questions. Get a native speaker to read the questions and answer them. Get someone proficient to translate the questions into the first language of the learners to see if they mean the same when they are translated. The questions in the *Return Ticket, Please!* example use simple language and language from the text.

Validity

- Answering the questions should require reading of the text. Sometimes it is possible to answer questions from background knowledge. Sometimes the choices in multiple-choice or true/false questions make it obvious which choice is likely to be the correct answer. To check if the questions require reading of the text, ask a very proficient reader, perhaps a native speaker, to answer the questions without having read the text. Getting that person to think aloud while answering the questions can be very revealing and can be a good guide to the particular changes that need to be made to each question. A few of the questions in the *Return Ticket, Please!* example can be answered by our well-informed person without reading the text, for example questions 1, 4 and 7. Question 3 about "trundled" could also be answered by a person with a very rich vocabulary, but this word is well beyond the eighth 1,000 word level. Several of the questions, however, require a careful reading of the text. Question 2 requires understanding the implications of "first". Question 6 requires reading and understanding the text and making inferences.
- The question should not use the exact words used in the text. If the question repeats part of a sentence from the text, the learners may be able to answer it in a cut-and-paste fashion without truly understanding the text. Questions that paraphrase the text will be more challenging to answer and will require understanding of both the text and the questions. The danger is that because different words are used in the questions, the questions may involve vocabulary and grammar that is more difficult than the text. Questions 1, 6, 7 and 8 all involve words that are paraphrases of what is in the text.
- The questions should measure reasonable comprehension. This means that the questions should not focus on items of small detail that a proficient native speaker would not remember from the text. The questions should measure comprehension not memory. They should also not require calculations or logical deduction that goes beyond normal comprehension. To check this, ask a highly proficient learner,

or a native speaker, to read the text and answer the questions. They should get all the answers correct. Filling in the information transfer table for the *Return Ticket, Please!* text involves quite detailed knowledge from the text and would best be answered by looking back at the text. Similarly, short answer questions 1 and 3 require information that might not be easily remembered without looking back at the text.

- The sequence of the questions should not make it more difficult to answer them. Usually the order of the questions should be in the same order as the information occurs in the text. Some researchers argue that global questions focusing on the main idea and overall understanding should come before questions on detail. This is not easy to check, but getting a highly proficient reader to read the text and answer the questions while thinking aloud can help with this. The order of the questions in the *Return Ticket, Please!* example follows the order of the ideas in the text.

Practicality

- The test should be set out so that marking is easy to do. If all the places to write the answers to a true/false test are lined up on the right-hand side of the answer sheet, marking can easily be done using an answer key which is held against the side of the page. If a space is provided for each short answer, then it is easy to find the answers and they will all be in the right order. Skill at designing an answer sheet comes with experience, but spending time carefully looking at the design can save a lot of marking time. To check this, see how long it takes to mark the test and how much page turning and searching is required when marking.

Some of the guidelines above need not be followed if there is a good reason. For example, in a speed reading course it is usually a good idea to have several easy questions that could be answered without reading the text. This encourages the learner to keep reading faster without being over-concerned with detailed comprehension issues. Similarly, very difficult questions could be set if the reading has an application goal; that is, if the purpose of the reading is for the learner to apply information from the text to solve a problem. In general, however, it is worth checking comprehension tests to see that they meet the above guidelines. For a further discussion of reliability, validity and practicality, see Nation and Newton (2009) *Teaching ESL/EFL Listening and Speaking*.

## Issues in Making and Using Reading Comprehension Tests

There are several issues that are of concern in the construction and use of reading comprehension tests.

### Should the Test Consist of One Text or Several Shorter Texts?

A major reason for using several texts is to try to reduce the effects of background knowledge on the test. If a learner happens to know a lot about the topic of the text, they are much more likely to do better on a comprehension test on that text. If several texts on different topics are used, this reduces the likely effect of background knowledge because any one learner is unlikely to have good background knowledge of all the texts in the test.

A second reason for using a range of texts is to make the test more representative of the different genres of texts that the learners will have to read in their normal use of the language. A third reason is so that there can be several questions each focusing on the same kind of information. For example, if the test is to measure skill in finding the main idea of a text, the test will be more valid if there are several texts each with its own main idea question.

### Should the Time Allowed to Sit a Reading Comprehension Test be Limited?

Obviously, tests cannot be allowed to go on hour after hour, but in general if the aim of the test is to measure skill, it is best if learners have plenty of time to demonstrate this skill. Sometimes the distinction is made between a power test and a speed test. In a power test, learners have largely unrestricted time to show what they can do. A power test where many learners do not have enough time to answer every question is not going to provide a meaningful result.

### Should Learners be Allowed to Look Back at the Text when they Answer the Questions?

If learners are not allowed to look back at the text, then the test involves a strong element of skill in remembering. When looking at the results of such a test, we do not know if a poor score is the result of poor comprehension, poor memory or both.

It could be argued that for some kinds of reading it is important to be able to remember the main ideas of what has been read. If a teacher wants to include this skill in a test, then there should not be too many questions on each text, probably no more than four or five. The questions should also focus on what someone could sensibly be expected to remember, such as the main idea and main points rather than very detailed parts of the text.

*Should Learners be Allowed to Use Dictionaries?*

Studies of the factors involved in reading usually show that vocabulary knowledge is the major component in reading comprehension. Thus, as a general rule, dictionary use should not be allowed during a reading comprehension test. Passages which are appropriate to the level of the learners need to be used. However, if the aim of the test is to find out how well learners can read a particular type of difficult text with assistance, then dictionaries could be allowed. Studies of dictionary use in writing have shown that quite a large proportion of the time is spent consulting the dictionary. If dictionary use takes a lot of time away from reading and considering the questions, dictionary use may interfere with measuring comprehension.

*Should the Questions be in the First Language and should the Learners be Allowed to Answer in the First Language?*

The idea behind allowing learners to use the first language to answer questions is that this is more likely to directly measure comprehension. When the learners have to read second language questions and write their answers in the second language, comprehension of questions and second language writing skill are playing a part in measuring comprehension. Do the learners make poor answers because of poor reading comprehension of the text, poor comprehension of the questions, poor skill in writing answers in the second language, or any combination of these? If the learners feel comfortable with first language questions they could be worth using.

*When Marking Comprehension Questions Requiring Written Answers, should Learners be Penalised for Poor Spelling, Poor Punctuation, and Poor Grammar?*

Reading comprehension tests are supposed to measure reading comprehension. Other skills and knowledge, particularly skill in writing, should not get in the way of this measurement. If they do, the validity of the test is affected. It is no longer a true measure of reading comprehension. For this reason, learners should not be penalised for poor written production as long as what they write can be understood.

# CHAPTER 7

# Helping Learners Write

## Principles for Teaching Writing

The following principles can be used to evaluate teaching and learning activities so that the best are chosen for use. The principles can also be used to evaluate a writing course or the writing section of a language course to make sure that learners are getting a good range of opportunities for learning. Within each strand the principles are ranked with the most important principle first.

*Meaning-focused Input*

- Learners should bring experience and knowledge to their writing. Writing is most likely to be successful and meaningful for the learners if they are well prepared for what they are going to write. This preparation can be done through the choice of topic, or through previous work done on the topic either in the first or second language. We will look at experience tasks later in this chapter.

*Meaning-focused Output*

- Learners should do lots of writing and lots of different kinds of writing. There are many elements of the writing skill which are peculiar to writing and so time spent writing provides useful practice for these elements. This is a very robust principle for each of the four skills. Different genres use different writing conventions and draw on different language features (Biber, 1989) and so it is useful to make sure that learners are getting writing practice in the range of genres that they will have to write in. Chapter 9 on topic types describes one approach to different kinds of writing.

- Learners should write with a message-focused purpose. Most writing should be done with the aim of communicating a message to the reader and the writer should have a reader in mind when writing. In the following chapters we will look at ways of doing this.
- Writing should interest learners and draw on their interests.
- Learners should experience a feeling of success in most of their writing.
- Learners should use writing to increase their language knowledge. The section on guided tasks in this chapter focuses on this.
- Learners should develop skill in the use of computers to increase the quality and speed of their writing. As we shall see, computers provide very useful ways of providing feedback, especially when the learners submit their writing as a computer file.
- Writing instruction should be based on a careful needs analysis which considers what the learners need to be able to do with writing, what they can do now, and what they want to do.

*Language-focused Learning*

- Learners should know about the parts of the writing process and should be able to discuss them in relation to their own and others' writing. Chapter 8 focuses on the writing process.
- Learners should have conscious strategies for dealing with parts of the writing process.
- Where the L1 uses a different script or where learners are not literate in their L1, the learners should give attention to clarity and fluency in producing the form of the written script. Such activities can include careful writing, copying models, and doing repetitive writing movements (see Chapter 2).
- Spelling should be given an appropriate amount of deliberate attention largely separated from feedback on writing. We have already looked at the teaching and learning of spelling in Chapter 2.
- Teachers should provide and arrange for feedback that encourages and improves writing. Chapter 10 looks at responding to written work.
- Learners should be aware of the ethical issues involved in writing.

*Fluency Development*

- Learners should increase their writing speed so that they can write very simple material at a reasonable speed. Fluency development can occur through repetitive activities and through working with easy, familiar material. The following section looks at how tasks can be designed.

For another similar list of principles see Grabe and Kaplan (1996), pp. 261–264.

## Designing Tasks

Imagine that a teacher wishes to help learners in her class improve their writing skills. To do this she will get them to work on writing tasks that will take them beyond their present level of proficiency. But to make sure that the learners are successful in doing the tasks, she may have to provide some help. There are several ways in which she could do this.

1. She could think of a topic that the learners are very familiar with, such as a recent exciting event. She then gets the learners talking about the event so that the ideas and the organisation of the ideas are clear and so that the learners have an oral command of the language needed to describe the event. When all this previous knowledge has been stimulated, the learners are then told to put it in writing. As the ideas, organisation and necessary language are all familiar to them, the learners have only to concentrate on turning these ideas into a written form.
2. The teacher could think of a topic and then put the learners into groups of three or four. Each group has to plan and produce one piece of writing. By helping each other, the learners in each group are able to produce a piece of writing that is better than any one of them could have produced by working alone.
3. The teacher finds or makes a guided composition exercise, such as a series of pictures with accompanying questions and useful language items.
4. The teacher chooses a topic and then lets the learners get on with their writing. They may ask for help if they need it, but they are mainly left to work independently.

These four kinds of tasks are called experience tasks, shared tasks, guided tasks, and independent tasks.

One way to look at these types of tasks is to see their job as dealing with the gap which exists between learners' present knowledge and the demands of the learning task. Experience tasks try to narrow the gap as much as possible by using or developing learners' previous experience. Shared tasks try to get learners to help each other cross the gap. Guided tasks try to bridge the gap by providing the support of exercises and focused guidance. Independent tasks leave learners to rely on their own resources.

## Experience Tasks

A very effective way of making a task easier is to make sure that the learners are familiar with as many parts of it as possible. This has several effects. First, it makes sure that learners are not overloaded by having to think about several different things at the same time. Second, it allows the learners the chance to concentrate on the part of the task that they need to learn. Third, it helps the learners perform a normal language activity in a normal way with a high chance of success.

## Bringing Tasks Within the Learners' Experience

One of the most common examples of an experience task in foreign language learning is the use of graded readers. Once learners have a vocabulary of 300 words or more, they should be able to read Stage 1 graded readers because these are written within that vocabulary level. Normally, such learners would not be able to read books written in English because unsimplified texts would be far too difficult for them. However, because Stage 1 graded readers use vocabulary that is familiar to the learners, use familiar sentence patterns, and involve simple types of stories, elementary learners are able to read Stage 1 readers without too much difficulty and with a feeling of success. The task of reading a graded reader is made easier because the writer of the graded reader has brought many of the parts of the task within the learners' experience.

In Chapter 2 we saw another way of doing this for reading which is often used in New Zealand primary schools. The teacher sits with a learner who has just drawn a picture. The learner tells the teacher the story of the picture and the teacher writes down the learner's story in the learner's words. This story then becomes the learner's reading text. It is not difficult for the learner to read because the language, the ideas in the story, and the sequence of ideas in the story are all within the learner's experience. The unfamiliar part of the task, which is also the learning goal of the activity, is the decoding of the written words.

Here is an example of how a writing task could be brought within the learners' experience. The learners are given a task to do which involves some reading and a following problem-solving activity that they have to write up. After doing the reading, the learners get together in first language groups and discuss the reading and the activity they will have to do in their first language. When they are satisfied that they have a clear understanding of what needs to be done, they then individually do the activity and write it up in English. The discussion in the first language makes sure that they truly understand the knowledge needed to do the task and the nature of the task.

There are several ways of presenting or controlling a task so that much of it is within the learners' experience.

## Making Sure Learners have the Experience to do a Task

If learners do not have enough experience to do a task, then either the task can be changed so that it is brought within their experience, or the learners can be provided with the experience which will help them do the task. A common way of providing learners with experience is to take them on a visit or field trip. For example, the teacher may take the class to a fire station. While they are there, they find out as much as they can about the fire station. They may even have a set of questions to answer. After the visit the writing task should be easier because the learners have experienced the ideas that they will write about, they have used or heard the language items that they need in the writing task, and they can choose how they will organise the writing. Their only difficulty should be putting the ideas into a written form and this is the learning goal for the task.

Learners may already have experience that they can draw on, but they are not aware of the relevance of this experience or their knowledge of the experience is largely unorganised. By discussing and sharing experience, learners can prepare themselves for certain tasks.

A more formal way of providing learners with experience to do a task is by pre-teaching. For example, before the learners read a text, the teacher can teach them the vocabulary they will need, can give them practice in finding the main idea, or can get them to study some of the ideas that will occur in the text.

Table 7.1 shows the three main ways of making sure learners have the experience needed to do a particular task.

Experience tasks are ones where the learners already have a lot of

**Table 7.1** Ways of Providing Experience

| | |
|---|---|
| Control through selection or simplification | Using simplified material |
| | Using carefully graded material |
| | Using learner produced material |
| | Using material based on first language material |
| Recall or sharing of previous experience | Discussions and brainstorming |
| | Questioning peers |
| Pre-teaching or experiencing | Direct teaching of sounds, vocabulary, grammar, text types . . . |
| | Visits and field trips |
| | Direct teaching of content |

the knowledge needed to do the task. Preparation for experience tasks thus involves choosing topics that the learners already know a lot about, providing learners with knowledge and experience to use in their writing and, through discussion, stimulating previous knowledge relevant to the writing task. Here are some experience tasks for writing.

In **draw and write** the learners draw a picture about something that happened to them or something imagined, and then they write about it, describing the picture. The picture provides a way of recalling past experience and acts as a memory cue for the writing.

**Linked skills** tasks are the commonest kinds of fluency task. The writing task is set as the final activity in a series that involves speaking about, then listening to and then reading about the topic. By the time they get to the writing task, the learners have a very large amount of content and language experience to draw on. Such linked skills activities fit easily into theme based work (Nation and Gu, 2007).

In **partial writing**, working together the learners list useful words that they will need in the following writing task.

**Ten perfect sentences** involves the teacher showing the learners a picture or suggesting an easy subject like my family, cars, etc., and the learners must write ten separate sentences about that. They are given one mark for each correct sentence.

At the beginning of a course, each learner chooses a topic that they will research and keep up-to-date each week during the course. This recording of information is their **issue log**. At regular intervals they give talks to others about their topic and prepare written reports.

**Setting your own questions** is an amusing activity. Each student produces the question they want to write about. This is then translated into good English and is made into an examination question which the students answer under examination conditions (McDonough, 1985).

### Shared Tasks

A task which is too difficult for an individual to do alone may be done successfully if a pair or group does it. A well-known example is group composition where three or four learners work together to produce a piece of writing that is superior to what any one of the group could do alone. There are several reasons why this happens, particularly in second language learning. First, although learners may be of roughly equal proficiency, they will certainly have learnt different aspects of the language (Saragi et al., 1978). Second, although learners may know a particular language item, they may find difficulty in accessing it. The prompting and help of others may allow them to do this. Third, where groups contain learners of differing proficiency, there is the opportunity for more personalised teaching to occur with one learner working with another who needs help.

Many experience tasks and guided tasks can be done in a group, thus increasing the help that learners are given with the tasks.

Most shared tasks have the advantages of requiring little preparation by the teacher, reducing the teacher's supervision and marking load, and encouraging the learners to see each other as a learning resource.

When doing a **reproduction exercise** the learners read or listen to a story and then they retell it without looking at the original. This type of composition is easier if the learners are allowed to read or listen to the story several times, before they write it. The teacher can tell the learners to try to write the story so that it is very similar to the original, or to add extra details and make changes if they wish. The same technique can be used with spoken instead of written input. The teacher reads a story to the class. After they have listened to the story, they must write it from their memory. If the teacher wants to give the learners a lot of help, the teacher reads the story several times, but not so many times that the learners can copy it exactly. As the learners cannot remember all the words of the story, they have to make up parts of it themselves. This gives them practice in composition. This exercise is sometimes called a **dicto-comp** (Ilson, 1962; Riley, 1972; Nation, 1991), because it is half-way between dictation and composition. Marking is easy.

The exercise can be made more difficult to suit the abilities of the learners. Here are three different ways of doing this, the second way is more difficult then the first, and the third is more difficult than the second.

1. The teacher reads a short passage several times.
2. The teacher reads a long passage once or twice. The learners can take notes while the passage is being read.
3. The learners listen to the passage once. When they write they must try to copy the style of the original (Mitchell, 1953).

This activity is called a **dicto-gloss** (Wajnryb, 1988 and 1989) if it is done as group work and if the learners take notes during two listening sessions.

To make a **blackboard composition** the whole class works together. The teacher or the learners suggest a subject and a rough plan for the composition. Members of the class raise their hands and suggest a sentence to put in the composition. If the sentence is correct it is written on the blackboard. If it is not correct, the class and the teacher correct it and then it is written on the board. In this way the composition is built up from the learners' suggestions and the learners' and the teacher's corrections. When the whole composition is finished, the learners read it and then it is rubbed off the blackboard. The learners do not copy it in their books before this. Then the learners must rewrite it from memory. This last part can be done as homework (Radford, 1969). The teacher has only to prepare a subject. Marking is easy as the learners usually make very few mistakes when rewriting.

The learners are divided into groups for **group-class composition**. The teacher gives the subject of the composition and then the learners in their groups discuss and make a list of the main ideas that they will write about. Then the teacher brings the class together and, following the learners' suggestions, makes a list of the main ideas on the blackboard. After this is discussed, the learners return to their groups and write a composition as a group. When the composition is finished each member of the group makes a copy of the composition. Only one copy is handed to the teacher for marking. The learners correct their copies by looking at the marked copy when the teacher gives it back to them. It is useful if they discuss the teacher's corrections in their groups.

In **group composition**, the learners are divided into groups or pairs. Each group writes one composition. Each learner suggests sentences and corrects the sentences suggested by the other learners. When the composition is finished, each learner makes a copy but only one composition from each group is handed to the teacher to be marked. When the composition has been marked, the learners correct their own copy from the marked one. The teacher just has to suggest a subject. Marking is usually easy because the learners correct most of the mistakes themselves before the composition is handed to the teacher. The teacher marks only one composition for each group.

When **writing with a secretary**, the learners work in pairs to do a piece of writing. One member of the pair has primary responsibility for the content and the other has to produce the written form.

### Guided Tasks

Most coursebooks make tasks easier by using exercises that carefully guide the learners. This usually has the effect of narrowing the task that the learners have to do. For example, guided composition exercises, such as picture composition, provide the ideas that the learners will write about. The exercises often provide needed vocabulary and structures and determine how the piece of writing will be organised. The learners' job is to compose the sentences that make up the composition. Guided tasks provide a lot of support for the learners *while* they do the task. This has several effects.

1. First, as we have seen, the task is narrowed. That is, the learners only do a part of the work that would normally be required in such an

activity. This is good if that part of the task is worth focusing on and helps learners achieve a useful learning goal. It is not good if the narrowed task results in learners doing things that bear little relation to the normal wider task. Substitution exercises have often been criticised for this reason.

2. A second effect of the support given during guided tasks is that it allows grading and sequencing of tasks. Experience tasks require the teacher to be sensitive to learners' familiarity with parts of a task and to provide and stimulate previous experience where necessary. Guided tasks, on the other hand, are designed so that guidance is provided as a part of the activity. It does not have to be provided by the teacher. For this reason, most coursebooks for English language teaching contain a lot of guided tasks. For the same reason, teachers may be reluctant to make their own guided tasks because of the amount of skill and work that has to go into making them.

3. A third effect of the support given during guided tasks is the high degree of success expected. If learners make errors in guided tasks this is often seen as a result of a poorly made task; that is, the guidance was not sufficient.

There are several types of guided tasks which can work at the level of the sentence, paragraph or text.

*Identification*

In identification techniques the learners are guided by being presented with an item which they must repeat, translate, or put in a different form with a related meaning to show that they have understood or correctly perceived the item, or to show that they can produce the related foreign language item. Dictation, copying, and writing from information transfer diagrams are identification techniques. Identification techniques can also include translation from the first language.

In **translation** the learners translate sentences or a story into English. This exercise is easier if the story is specially prepared by the teacher so that it contains very few translation problems.

With **look and write** the teacher performs an action, or shows the learners a picture of a real object, and the learners write a sentence to describe what they see. This is easier for the learners if the teacher gives them an example of the sentence pattern.

For **picture composition** the teacher shows the learners a picture or a series of pictures. Under the picture there are several questions. By answering the questions with the help of the picture, the learners can write a composition. If the teacher wishes to make it easier for the learners, the learners can answer the questions aloud around the class before they do any writing.

The **delayed copying** technique is designed to help learners become fluent in forming letters and words, especially where the writing system of the second language is different from that of the first language. It also helps learners develop fluent access to phrases. The learners have a paragraph on a piece of paper next to them. They look at a phrase, try to remember it, then look away and write it. They should only look at each phrase once, and they should try to break the work into phrases that are as long as they can manage (Hill, 1969). This exercise is even better if the learners pause while not looking at the passage before they write the phrase. This delay accustoms them to holding English phrases in their head. This technique is similar to the read-and-look-up technique (West, 1960: 12–13) and could be called the look-up and write technique. Copying letter by letter, or word by word is of little value in improving a learner's knowledge of English. Any passage that contains known words and sentence patterns can be used for delayed copying.

*Understanding Explanations*

In some techniques the learners follow explanations and descriptions and act on them. Here are some examples. (1) The teacher explains a grammar rule to help the learners make correct sentences following a rule. The teacher says, "When we use <u>going to</u> to talk about the future, <u>going to</u> is followed by the stem form of the verb, for example, <u>I am going to see it</u>. The subject of the sentence should agree with the verb <u>to be</u> which comes in front of <u>going to</u>. Now you make some sentences using <u>going to</u>." (2) The teacher tells the learners a rule, for example a spelling rule or a rule about singular countable nouns, and the learners apply the rule to some material.

**Writing with grammar help** involves guided compositions which are based on special grammar problems. Usually the rules are given first for the learner to study and then they must use the rules when doing the composition. Here is an example based on countable and uncountable nouns. The first part just deals with countable nouns. The second part deals with uncountable nouns and the third part mixes both together. Only part one is shown here. Other exercises like this can be made for verb groups, joining words, *a* and *the*, and so on.

---

**Countable nouns**
1. Countable nouns can be singular or plural.
2. A singular countable noun must have *a*, or *the*, or a word like this, *my*, *each*, *every*, *Fred's* in front of it.

3. *Many, several, both, a few, these, those, two, three,* etc. are only used in front of plural countable nouns.
4. *Each, every, a, another, one* are only used in front of singular countable nouns.
5. *People* is a plural countable noun.

**Uncountable nouns**
1. Uncountable nouns cannot be plural.
2. Sometimes an uncountable noun does not need *the, this,* etc. in front of it.
3. *Much* is only used in front of uncountable nouns.

**Part 1**
All these words are countable nouns. Put them in the correct place in the story. You must use some of the words more than once. Follow the rules for countable nouns.

*language, country, word, kind, world, people, dictionary.*

_____ living in different _____ use different _____ of words. Today there are about 1,500 different _____ in the _____. Each _____ has many _____. A very big English dictionary has four or five hundred thousand words. Nobody knows or uses every _____ in a dictionary like this. To read most books you need to know about five or six thousand words. The words that you know are called your vocabulary. You should try to make your vocabulary bigger. Read as many _____ as you can. There are many _____ in easy English for you to read. When you meet a new _____, find it in your _____.

To make this exercise, the teacher finds a story that is not too difficult for the learners, and takes out certain words.

*Answering Questions*

In some guided tasks the guidance comes through questions. True/false statements are included in this type. Questions can be asked or answered in the first language. For example, in some reading courses where writing is not taught, questions on the reading passage are written in English but the learners answer in their first language. The questions can also be asked or answered by means of pictures and diagrams. Learners can take the teacher's place and ask the questions while the teacher or other learners answer them. There is a wide variety of question forms and types. Stevick's (1959) excellent article on teaching techniques describes some of these.

In **answer the questions** the teacher writes several questions on the blackboard. These questions are based on a story that the learners have just heard or read, or have heard or read several days ago. The answers to the questions give the main ideas of the story. The learners answer the questions and add extra ideas and details if they are able to. The composition is easier if the learners have heard or read the story recently and if there are many questions.

It is easy for the teacher to make the questions because they can be closely based on the original story. When marking the teacher should allow the learners to change and add things as they wish. The composition can be based on the learners' own experience or can ask them to use their imagination. The more questions there are, the easier the composition is. Here is an example.

*Good and Bad Guests*
Do people sometimes visit your house? Who are they? Do they sometimes stay at your house for several days? Do you sometimes stay at other people's houses? Do you find that you enjoy having some guests, but that you do not enjoy having certain others? What sorts of people do you like as guests? What sorts of people do you dislike as guests? What sorts of things make a person a good guest? What ones make a person a bad guest? (from Hill, 1966, p. 35).

*Correction*

In correction techniques the learners look for mistakes either in ideas or form and describe them or correct them. They include techniques like finding grammar mistakes in sentences, finding unnecessary and unusual words which have been put in a reading passage, finding wrong facts in a reading passage, finding the word that does not go with the others in a group of words, describing inappropriate items in pictures, and so on. Learners show that they have found mistakes by

- underlining or circling them
- writing the corrected item.

*Completion*

In completion techniques the learners are given words, sentences, a passage, or pictures that have parts missing or that can have parts added to them. The learners complete the words, sentences or passage by filling in the missing parts, or by saying what is missing from the picture.

For **complete the sentences** the learners are given sentences with words missing. They must put the correct words with the correct form in the empty spaces. A few words can fill all the empty spaces. This type of exercise is used to practice *a* or *the; some, any,* etc.; prepositions, etc. The missing words can be given at the beginning of the exercise.

*Put **at**, **on**, or **in** in the empty spaces.*
1. He arrived _____ ten o'clock.
2. The meeting begins _____ Friday.
3. My uncle died _____ July.
4. My birthday is _____ 21st January.
5. It begins _____ midnight.

In another form of the exercise each missing word is given but the learners must use the correct form. This type of exercise is used to practise tense, verb groups, singular/plural, pronouns, questions, etc.

1. One of the _____ was there. (boy)
2. Every _____ tried to get as many as possible. (person)

When verb groups are being practised the learner sometimes has to add other words.

1. _____ you _____ to leave now? (want)
2. _____ you _____ him last week? (meet)

Some explanation of the grammar can be given at the beginning of the exercise.

In **backwriting** the learners read a passage. After they have understood the text, they copy some of the key words from the passage onto a sheet of paper. Only the base form of the word is copied (i.e. *walk* not *walking*). The learners then put the text away and write what they remember of the passage filling in around the key words that they copied.

## *Ordering*

In ordering techniques the learners are presented with a set of items in the wrong order which they must rearrange in the desired order. For example, the learners are presented with a set of letters *o k o b*. They must rearrange these letters to make a word, *book*. Words can be rearranged to make a sentence, sentences to make a passage, pictures to make a story, and so on. Ordering techniques can easily be combined with other types of actions. For example, the learners are presented with a set of letters that can be rearranged to make an English word. The learners respond by giving the first language translation of the word.

With **put the words in order** the learners are given sentences with the words in the wrong order. They must rewrite them putting the words in the correct order.

is city it very a important

**Follow the model** shows the learners a pattern and gives them a list of words. They must use the words to make sentences that follow the same pattern as the model.

He made them cry.
saw  I  laugh  let  she  go  her  fight  heard  him

Instead of all the words, just the content words can be provided.

Some ordering techniques, like the examples given above, can be done without the learners referring to any other clues. Other ordering techniques contain extra information so that the learners can do the ordering correctly. For example, the learners are given a set of words. The teacher reads the words quickly in a different order and while listening to this information the learners number or put the words in the same order as the teacher says them. Here is another example. After the learners have read a passage, they are given a set of sentences containing the main points in the message. The learners must put these sentences in the right order so that the order of the main points in the sentences is the same as the order in the passage.

*Substitution*

In substitution techniques the learners replace one or more parts of a word, sentence, passage, picture, story, etc. So, the input of a substitution technique has two parts, the frame which contains the part where the substitution must be made, for example a word, sentence, etc., and the item which fits into the frame. So, if the frame is a sentence, *He seldom goes there.*, the teacher can give the item *often* which is substituted for *seldom* in the frame to give the response *He often goes there.*

The learners can write sentences from a **substitution table**.

| 1 | 2 | 3 | 4 |
|---|---|---|---|
| He | said | | it was not a problem. |
| They | agreed | that | it was the right time. |
| I | decided | | nothing could be done. |
| We | pretended | | |

The substitution table gives the learners the chance to practise making correct sentences, and to see different words that can be in each place in the sentence (George, 1965).

In **What is it?** the teacher writes some sentences on the blackboard. The sentences describe something or someone. Here is one plan (Nation, 1978).

It is <u>thin</u>.
It is <u>black</u>.
It has <u>many teeth</u>.
It is made of <u>plastic</u>.
We can find it <u>near a mirror</u>.
It costs <u>a pound</u>.
<u>Everybody</u> uses it.
It is used for <u>combing your hair</u>.
What is it?

The teacher shows the learners how to change the sentences to talk about different things. While he does this the teacher follows the plan very closely. For example, <u>a needle</u>.

It is thin.
It is silver.
It has a sharp point.
It is made of steel.
We can find it in our house.
It costs five pence.
You need good eyes to use it.
It is used for sewing things.
What is it?

Then the teacher gives the learners the name of something, for example <u>a pen</u>, and they must describe it using the plan. He gives a few new words if they are needed in the description. Each learner can be given a different thing to describe. When the learners know how to follow the plan, it can be played as a game. One learner writes a description of something and then the others try to guess what it is. As they improve, the learners can add some sentences that are not in the plan and make other changes.

The exercise can be made more controlled by asking the learners to follow the sentence patterns of the plan very carefully. It can be made freer by telling the learners to add any sentences that they need to make their description. Thus, everybody in the class can do the exercise with the better learners doing it in an almost free way and with the others doing the exercise in a very controlled way.

### Transformation

In transformation techniques the learners have to rewrite or say words, sentences, or passages by changing the grammar or organisation of the form of the input. This type of technique also includes rewriting passages, substitution where grammar changes are necessary, and joining two or more sentences together to make one sentence.

In **change the sentence** the learners are given some sentences and are asked to rewrite them making certain changes. Here are some examples.

*Rewrite these sentences using the past tense.*
1. He wants to see me.
2. Do you like it?

*Make these sentences passive. Do not use the subject of the active sentence in the passive sentence.*
The arrow wounded him. He was wounded.
1. Some people pushed her over the bank.
2. The noise frightened her.

For **join the sentences (sentence combining)** the learners are given pairs of sentences. They must join together the two sentences to make one sentence. This type of exercise is used to practise conjunctions, adjectives + to + stem, relative clauses, etc. Here are some examples.

This coffee is hot. I can't drink it.
This coffee is too hot to drink.

1. She is still young. She can't marry you.
2. He is tired. He can't go.

I met the man. You talked about him before.
I met the man who you talked about before.

1. Your friend is waiting near the shop. The shop is next to the cinema.
2. I will lend you the book. You wanted it.

There has been a lot of first language research on sentence combining generally showing positive effects (Hillocks, 1984; Hillocks, 1991). The motivation for sentence combining for first language learners is that the most reliable measure of first language writing development is a measure related to the number of complex sentences (the T-unit). Sentence combining is thus seen as a way of focusing directly on this aspect of writing development.

In **writing by steps** the learners are given a passage. They must add certain things to it, or make other changes. Here is an example from Dykstra, Port and Port (1966). The same passage can be used several times for different exercises at different levels of difficulty.

---

**Why the Hyena has Stripes (Part 1)**

[1] Ananse, the spider, and his neighbour, the hyena, decided to go to the river together. [2] There they met the King of the river who presented them with a gift of many fish. [3] Ananse and the hyena made a fire, and as Ananse cooked the fish, he threw them over his shoulder on to the river bank to cool.

[4] H owever, the greedy hyena caught and ate all of them.

[5] When Ananse turned to eat his fish, tears of anger filled his eyes.

[6] The hyena asked the spider why he was weeping, but Ananse calmly replied that the smoke from the fire was in his eyes. [7] Nevertheless, he was already planning his revenge.

1. Copy.
2. Rewrite the entire passage changing the word <u>hyena</u> to <u>zebra</u> each time it appears.
3. Rewrite the entire passage changing <u>Ananse, the spider</u> to <u>the spiders</u>. (When either <u>Ananse</u> or <u>the spider</u> appears alone, change it to <u>the spiders</u>.) Remember to change both the verbs and pronouns whenever it is necessary to do so.
4. Rewrite the entire passage supplying adjectives before the words <u>spider</u>, <u>hyena</u>, and <u>river</u> (sentence[1]); <u>shoulder</u> (sentence[3]); <u>eyes</u> (sentence[5]); and <u>fire</u> (sentence[6]).
5. Rewrite the entire passage supplying your own verbal phrases at the beginning of the following sentences. Begin your phrase with the verb form given here: sentence[1] (having heard); sentence[3] (having agreed); sentence[6] (seeing).

---

In guided activities a large part of the writing has already been done for the learners and they focus on some small part that they must do. The activity provides support while learners do the writing.

With **marking guided writing** guided compositions can be marked by a group of learners using model answers before they are handed to the teacher. The teacher just checks to see that the learners have done the marking correctly.

## Independent Tasks

Independent tasks require the learners to work alone without any planned help. Learners can work successfully on independent tasks when they have developed some proficiency in the language and when they have command of helpful strategies. These strategies can develop from experience, shared, or guided tasks. Let us look at learners faced with a difficult independent reading task, such as writing an assignment.

1. *An experience approach.* The learners could write several drafts. During each rewriting, the learners have the experience gained from the previous writings and preparation.
2. *A shared approach.* The learners could ask the teacher or classmates for help when they need it.
3. *A guided approach.* The learners could guide their writing by asking questions, by using an information transfer diagram or a well worked out set of notes that they have prepared, or by finding a good example of the kind of writing they want to do.

A good independent task has the following features: (1) it provides a reasonable challenge, i.e. it has some difficulty but the learners can see that with effort they can do it; (2) it is a task that learners are likely to face outside the classroom.

The difference between an experience and independent task lies in the control and preparation that goes into an experience task. Experience tasks are planned so that learners are faced with only one aspect of the task that is outside their previous experience. Independent tasks do not involve this degree of control and learners may be faced with several kinds of difficulty in the same task.

## Using the Four Kinds of Tasks

The aim in describing the four kinds of tasks is to make teachers aware of the possible approaches to dealing with the gap between the learners' knowledge and the knowledge required to do a task, and to make them aware of the very large number of activities that can be made to help learners. When teachers are able to think of a variety of ways of dealing with a problem, they can then choose the ones that will work best in their class. Let us end by looking at another example of the range of tasks available in a particular situation.

Your learners need to write about land use in the Amazon basin. For several reasons this task will be difficult for them. There are new concepts to learn, there is new vocabulary, and the text should be written in a rather academic way. What can the teacher do to help the learners with this task?

The first step is to think whether an experience task is feasible. Can the teacher bring the language, ideas, needed writing skills, or text organisation within the experience of the learners? For example, is it possible to bring the language within the learners' proficiency by pre-teaching vocabulary or discussing the topic before going on to the writing? Is it possible to bring the ideas within the learners' experience by getting them to collect pictures and read short articles about the Amazon basin? Can the possible organisation of the text be outlined and explained to the learners? If these things are not possible or if more help is needed, then the teacher should look at making the writing a shared task.

The writing could be made into a shared task in several ways. The class work together doing a blackboard composition, or they form groups with each group working on a different aspect of the content. If this is not possible or further help is needed, guided help can be given.

Some of the simpler guided tasks could involve answering a detailed set of questions to write the text, completing a set of statements, adding detail to a text, writing descriptions of pictures of the Amazon, and turning an information transfer diagram into a text.

The distinctions made here between experience, shared and guided tasks are for ease of description and to make the range of possibilities clearer. Experience or guided tasks can be done in small groups as shared tasks, just as experience tasks may have some guided elements.

One purpose of this chapter is to make teachers aware of the variety of ways in which they can support learners in their writing. Another purpose has been to describe some major task types that teachers can use to give them access to the large range of possibilities that are available to them when they try to close the gap between their learners' proficiency and the demands of the learning tasks facing them. The job of these tasks is to help learners gain mastery over the language, ideas, language skills and types of discourse that are the goals of their study.

# CHAPTER 8

# The Writing Process

## The Parts of a Writing Programme

With writing, as with the other skills of listening, speaking and reading, it is useful to make sure that learners are involved in meaning-focused use, language-focused learning, and fluency development. It is also important to make sure that the uses of writing cover the range of uses that learners will perform in their daily lives. These can include filling forms, making lists, writing friendly letters and business letters, note-taking and academic writing. Each of these types of writing involves special ways of organising and presenting the writing and this presentation also deserves attention.

## Meaning-focused Writing

Writing is an activity that can usefully be prepared for by work in the other skills of listening, speaking and reading. This preparation can make it possible for words that have been used receptively to come into productive use. For example, in an English for academic purposes programme, learners can be involved in keeping **issue logs** which are a kind of **project work**. At the beginning of the programme each learner chooses a topic or issue that they will follow through the rest of the programme—for example, terrorism, rugby, or Burmese politics. They become the local expert on this topic. Each week they seek information on this subject, getting information from newspapers, TV reports, textbooks and magazines. They provide oral reports on latest developments to other members of their group, and make a written summary each week of the new information. The reading, listening and spoken presentation provide good support for the writing. Writing is easier if learners write from a strong knowledge base.

## The Parts of the Writing Process

One way of focusing attention on different aspects of writing is to look at writing as a process. One possible division of the writing process contains the following seven subprocesses.

- considering the goals of the writer
- having a model of the reader
- gathering ideas
- organising ideas
- turning ideas into written text
- reviewing what has been written
- editing.

There are several important points that can be made about these subprocesses.

1. They do not necessarily occur in a certain order. For some writers, organising ideas may occur after they have been written. For many writers there is movement from one stage to another in a continuous cycle.
2. The effects of these subprocesses can be seen in learners' writing and in their spoken comments while and after they write. Several studies (Raimes, 1985; Zamel, 1983; Arndt, 1987) have observed and analysed the performance of second language teachers' writing and have described typical behaviour of experienced and inexperienced writers in relation to the parts of the process.
3. Help and training can be provided for any of the subprocesses. The main goal of a process approach is to help learners improve their skills at all stages of the process. In this chapter, the descriptions of the techniques to improve skill in writing make use of the subprocesses to describe the subskills.
4. Awareness of the subprocesses can help teachers locate sources of difficulty that learners face in their writing. A learner may have no difficulty in gathering ideas but may experience great difficulty in turning these ideas into written text. Another learner may have difficulty in organising ideas to make an acceptable piece of formal writing but may have no difficulty in getting familiar and well-organised ideas written in a well-presented form.
5. There are many ways of dividing the process into subprocesses. From

the point of view of teaching techniques, the best division is the one that relates most closely to differences between teaching techniques.

The main idea behind a process approach is that it is not enough to look only at what the learners have produced. In order to improve their production, it is useful to understand how it was produced. Let us now look in detail at each of the seven subprocesses.

## Considering the Goals of the Writer and Model of the Reader

Written work is usually done for a purpose and for a particular audience. For example, a friendly letter may be written to keep a friend or relative informed of you and your family's activities. When a letter like this is written, the writer needs to keep the goal in mind as well as suiting the information and the way it is expressed to the person who will receive it.

Once again, an important way of encouraging writers to keep their goals and audience in mind is to provide them with feedback about the effectiveness of their writing. This feedback can be direct comment on the writing as a piece of writing or it can be a response to the message. For example, Rinvolucri (1983) suggests that the teacher and learners should write letters to each other with the teacher responding to the ideas rather than the form of the letter.

Teachers should also check their writing programme to make sure that learners are given practice in writing for a range of purposes to a range of readers. The following list, adapted from Purves, Sofer, Takala and Vahapassi (1984), indicates how wide this range can be.

*Purpose*
 to learn
 to convey, signal
 to inform
 to convince, persuade
 to entertain
 to maintain friendly contact
 to store information
 to help remember information

*Role*
 write as yourself
 write as some other person

*Audience*
 self
 specified individual

specified group
classmates
general public

*Type of writing*
a note or formal letter
a formal letter
résumé, summary, paraphrase
narrative
description
exposition, analysis, definition, classification
narrative, description, with evaluative comment
argument
literary
advertisement, media
journal writing

In **writing with immediate feedback** the writer sits next to a reader and as each sentence or paragraph is written, the writer gets feedback from the reader and they discuss what has been written and what might come next. The writer then writes the next paragraph and the discussion continues. This technique is especially useful when writing instructions or technical descriptions.

In **writing to your students** the teacher writes personal letters to each learner and they reply in writing. The only rule is each letter should offer the reader some new bit of information about the writer. This technique involves genuine communication between the teacher and the learners (Rinvolucri, 1983).

**Situational composition** is a type of free composition. A situation is created using an advertisement, a letter, a table of numbers, etc. The learners must do a piece of writing that suits the situation. The language and the way of writing must suit the situation (Sweeting, 1967; Wingfield and Swan, 1971). Here are a few examples.

- The learner is given a letter that must be answered.
- The learner is given some facts that must be written as a newspaper report.
- The learner is given some facts that must be written as a report of an experiment.

**Letter writing** can be an activity between members of the class. The class can be organised so that some people pretend that they are working in a bank, others are working in shops, a tourist agency, a factory, a building company, and a school. They write letters to each other about various things, asking for information, looking for jobs, complaining about something, and so on. Or one class can become pen-friends with another class in another town or country.

Learners research and write academic **assignments**. Learners need to be familiar with the form of assignments and the conventions for quoting and acknowledging reference sources. The use of a marking schedule can help learners with this if they see the schedule before they do the assignment. The marking schedule can include space for comments on handwriting, spelling and grammar, use of sub-headings, use and acknowledgement of sources, quality of organisation and quality of ideas.

## Gathering Ideas

Leibman-Kleine (1987) suggests that techniques for gathering ideas about a topic can be classified into three groups. The first group consists of open-ended, free-ranging activities where all ideas are considered or the learners follow whatever path their mind takes. Typical of these are **brainstorming** and **quickwriting**. These activities could be preceded by relaxation activities where learners are encouraged to use all their senses to explore a topic. The second group consists of systematic searching procedures such as **questioning** (who, why, where, when . . .) or filling in an information transfer diagram. In all cases the learners have set steps to follow to make sure they consider all the important parts of the topic. Research by Franken (1988) has shown that when learners are in command of the ideas in a topic, the grammatical errors are significantly reduced in their writing. The third group consists of techniques which help learners gather and organise ideas at the same time. These include using tree diagrams and concept diagrams or maps. These all involve arranging ideas into relationships, particularly according to importance and level of generality. One of the biggest blocks in writing is a lack of ideas. Techniques which help learners gather ideas will have good effects on all other aspects of their writing.

For **group brainstorming** the learners get together in small groups and suggest as many ideas about the writing topic that they can think of. At first no idea is rejected or criticised because it may lead to other ideas. One person in the group keeps a record of the ideas.

With **list making** before writing, each learner makes a list of ideas to include in the writing. After the list is made then the learner attempts to organise it and this may lead to additions to the list.

**Looping** is when each learner writes as quickly as possible on the topic for 4 or 5 minutes. Then they stop, read what they have written, think about it and write one sentence summarising it. Then they repeat the procedure once more.

**Cubing** is when the learners consider the topic from six angles: (1) describe it; (2) compare it; (3) associate it; (4) analyse it; (5) apply it; (6) argue for and against it. They note the ideas that each of these points of view suggest and decide which ones they will use in their writing. Other similar procedures include asking, "who, what, when, where, how, why". So, for the topic "Should parents hit their children?", the learners work in small groups and (1) describe what hitting involves, (2) compare it with other kinds of punishment, (3) associate it with other uses of physical force such as capital punishment, (4) analyse what cause–effect sequences are involved in hitting, (5) apply the idea of hitting to various age levels, and (6) make a two-part table listing the pluses and minuses of hitting. After doing this the learners should have a lot of ideas to organise and write about.

**Using topic type grids**. Information transfer diagrams based on topic types (Chapter 9) are a very useful way of gathering information before the writing is done (Franken, 1987). They can also be used as a checklist during writing.

**Reading like a writer** is when the learner reads an article or text like the one they want to write. While reading the learner writes the questions that the writer seemed to be answering. These questions must be phrased at a rather general level. For example, the first question that might be written when reading an article might be "Why are people interested in this topic?". The next might be "What have others said about this topic before?". After reading and making the questions, the learner then writes an article or text by answering those questions. The learners make concept diagrams or information trees to gather, connect and organise ideas about the topic they are going to write about.

With **add details** the teacher gives the learners several sentences that contain the main ideas of a story. Each sentence can become the main sentence in a paragraph. The learners add description and more detail. The learners can explain the main sentence in a general way and then give particular examples of the main ideas.

**Quickwriting (speed writing)** is used with the main purpose of helping learners produce ideas. It has three features, the learners concentrate on content, they do not worry about error or the choice of words, and they write without stopping (Jacobs, 1986). They can keep a record of their speed in words per minute on a graph.

For **expanding writing** the learners write their compositions on every second line of the page. When they have finished writing they count the number of words and write the total at the bottom of the page. Then they go over their writing using a different coloured pen and add more detail. They can make use of the blank lines while they do this. They then count the total number of words again. Further additions can be made using yet another coloured pen. The teacher can then check the work and get the learners to write out their final draft (Chambers, 1985).

## Organising Ideas

The way learners organise ideas gives them a chance to put their own point of view and their own thought into their writing, particularly in writing assignments and answering examination questions. Often the ideas to be included in an assignment do not differ greatly from one writer to another, but the way the ideas are organised can add uniqueness to the piece of writing. Two possible ways of approaching the organisation of academic writing is to rank the ideas according to a useful criterion or to classify the ideas into groups. The use of sub-headings in academic writing is a useful check on organisation.

With **projection into dialogue** the learners look at a model letter and list the questions that the writer of the letter seemed to be answering. They then use these questions to guide their own writing. After the learners can do this with model texts, they can apply the same procedure to their own writing to see if it is well organised (Robinson, 1987).

## Ideas to Text

Some learners are able to say what they want to write but have difficulty in putting it into written form. That is, they have problems in translating their ideas into text. Some learners can do this but are very slow. That is, they lack fluency in turning ideas to text. A possible cause is the difference between the writing systems of the learners' first language and the second language. Arab learners of English have greater difficulty in this part of the writing process than Indonesian or French learners do because of the different written script. If the learners' first language uses a different writing system from English, then there is value in practising the formal skills of forming letters of the alphabet and linking these letters together. There is also value in giving some attention to spelling.

Some learners will find problems even in saying what they want to write. One cause may be lack of practice in writing in any language. Each cause requires different techniques to deal with it and teachers need to consider how to discover the causes and how to deal with them.

## Reviewing

An important part of the writing process is looking back over what has been written. This is done to check what ideas have already been included in the writing, to keep the coherence and flow of the writing, to stimulate further ideas, and to look for errors. Poor writers do not review, or review only to look for errors. Chapter 10 looks at responding to written work.

One way of encouraging learners to review their writing is to provide them with **checklists** (or scales) containing points to look for in their writing. Research on writing indicates that such scales have a significant effect on improving the quality of written work (Hillocks, 1984).

In **peer feedback** learners read their incomplete work to each other to get comments and suggestions on how to improve and continue it. The learners can work in groups and read each other's compositions. They make suggestions for revising before the teacher marks the compositions (Dixon, 1986). Learners can be trained to give helpful comments and can work from a checklist or a list of questions (Pica, 1986).

### Editing

Editing involves going back over the writing and making changes to its organisation, style, grammatical and lexical correctness, and appropriateness. Like all the other parts of the writing process, editing does not occur in a fixed place in the process. Writers can be periodically reviewing what they write, editing it, and then proceeding with the writing. Thus, editing is not restricted to occurring after all the writing has been completed.

Learners can be encouraged to edit through the feedback that they get from their classmates, teacher and other readers. Such feedback is useful if it occurs several times during the writing process and is expressed in ways that the writer finds acceptable and easy to act on. Feedback that focuses only on grammatical errors will not help with editing of content. Teachers need to look at their feedback to make sure it is covering the range of possibilities. Using a marking sheet divided into several categories is one way of doing this. Figure 8.1 is such a sheet for learners writing university assignments. It encourages comment on features ranging from the legibility of the handwriting to the quality of the ideas and their organisation.

Name _____

Topic _____

*Assessment sheet for the curriculum design assignment*

Presentation and organisation

Coverage of the relevant aspects of curriculum design

Integration of experience and linking of the aspects

Possible improvements and overall impression

**Figure 8.1** Example Marking Sheet

Feedback to the writer provides a means of focusing attention on the language used in writing and on the writing skill. Note that feedback includes, but is broader than, correction. In order to make sure that this feedback is covering a suitable range of aspects of the writing task, it is useful to have some model or scheme on which to base the feedback. One way is to base the feedback on the parts of the writing process described above. That is, writers should receive comments on the ideas in their writing (Are there enough? Are they relevant?), the organisation of these ideas (Are they well organised? Does the organisation make the ideas clear and interesting?), the ways the ideas are expressed in the text (Is the language use appropriate? Is the language use clear?), and so on. Another way is to base the feedback on the various goals of language courses (Language, Ideas, Skills, Text). The value of having some model to base feedback on is that it makes sure that the feedback is not too narrowly focused on grammatical correction but covers a range of focuses. A useful way of guiding feedback is to use a feedback sheet that is divided into sections with a space for comments in each section.

There are various ways of organising feedback on writing, including feedback from the teacher, feedback from other learners, and self-reflection and feedback by the writer.

### Marking Using a Graph

When the learners have finished writing a composition, they should count the number of words they have written. To avoid miscounting, they should count up to 50, make a line like this / after the 50th word and then begin at one again. At the end of their composition they write the number of words they have written, e.g. 236 words. When the teacher marks the composition, she counts the number of mistakes, and calculates the average number of the mistakes in every one hundred words. This is done by dividing the number of mistakes by the number of words with the result expressed as a percentage.

By having this average mark for each composition, the learners can see if they are improving. They should put their mark on a graph. This makes the learners eager to improve. Their aim is to make their graph go down. Usually there is fast improvement at the beginning which slows down as the average number of mistakes becomes less.

### Marking Using a System

It is probably more useful for the learners if the teacher does not correct their mistakes but shows them where the mistake is and what type of mistake it is. To do this a marking system is needed. Here is a useful one for the most common mistakes.

| In the margin | Their meaning | In the sentence |
|---|---|---|
| A | *a, the,* plural | It is book |
| P | Punctuation | This is Johns book |
| S | Spelling | occurrence |
| T | Tense | I walk |
|  | Agreement | he go |
|  | Verb group | can going |
| V | Verb needed | he happy |

The signs at the side of the page show the type of mistake, and the signs in the sentences show where it is. The learners should correct their mistakes themselves after the teacher has marked them. In most compositions, at least half of the mistakes are usually things that the learners already know about. They are there mainly because of carelessness.

Self-correction helps to stop this. The learners should be encouraged to develop the habit of checking their work carefully before giving it to the teacher to be marked. A marking system helps them to do this by showing them their main weaknesses.

Giving attention to the writing process is a way of bringing about improvement in learners' writing by providing help at the various stages of the process, instead of focusing only on the finished product. A process approach is most suited to writing because it is a largely solitary, productive skill where there is plenty of time to observe and consider the parts of the process. However, a process approach can be applied to at least some parts of listening, speaking and reading skills.

## Diagnosing Control of the Parts of the Writing Process

An advantage of seeing writing as a process consisting of related parts is that a writer's control of each of the parts can be examined in order to see what parts are well under the writer's control and which need to be worked on. Poor control of some of the parts may lead to a poor performance on other parts of the process.

There are three ways of getting information about control of the parts

- looking closely at the written product, that is, the pieces of writing that the writer has already written
- questioning the writer
- observing the writer going through the process of writing.

Here we will look at the types of information that can be gathered by looking closely at the written product. For each part of the writing process, we will look at the kinds of questions a teacher can seek answers for by analysing a piece of writing.

## Diagnosing from the Written Product

*The Goals of the Writer*

The questions try to find out if the writer is writing with a communicative purpose. Poor performance in this part of the process is signalled by the lack of a cohesive purpose.

- Does the piece of writing have a clear goal, such as presenting a balanced picture of a situation, or convincing the reader of a point of view, or providing a clear description of a situation?
- Has the writer clearly stated the goal and is this statement a true reflection of what the piece of writing does?

*A Model of the Reader*

These questions try to find out if the writer has a clear and consistent picture of who he or she is writing for. Poor performance in this part of the process is signalled by inconsistent style, lack of detail where the reader needs it and too much information where the reader already knows it.

- Is the degree of formality or informality consistent throughout the piece of writing?
- Is the amount of detail suited to the knowledge that the reader will bring to the text?
- If the writing is based on a set question, does the degree of formality in the writing match the level of formality in the question?

*Gathering Ideas*

These questions try to find out if the writer has included enough ideas in the piece of writing. Poor performance in this part of the process is the result of not having enough to say.

- Does the piece of writing contain plenty of relevant, interesting ideas?
- Does the range of ideas provide a suitably complete coverage of the parts of the topic?
- Does the piece of writing draw on a range of sources of information, for example personal opinion or experience, information gathered from reading, or original data?

*Organising Ideas*

These questions try to find out if the piece of writing is well organised. Poor performance in this part of the process results in a piece of writing that is difficult to follow, that does not try to grab the reader's attention, and that is annoyingly unpredictable.

- Are there clear parts to the piece of writing?
- Are these parts arranged in a way that is logical and interesting?
- Are the parts clearly signalled through the use of sub-headings or promises to the reader?
- Would it be easy to add sensible, well-sequenced sub-headings to the piece of writing?

*Ideas to Text*

These questions try to find out if the writer is able to express his or her ideas fluently and clearly. Poor performance in this part of the process is signalled by a short piece of writing, poorly expressed sentences, a large number of spelling, grammar and vocabulary errors, and a poorly connected piece of writing.

- How much was written in the time allowed?
- Are the ideas well expressed and easy to follow?
- Are the parts of the piece of writing clearly signalled?
- Is the writing largely error free?

*Reviewing*

These questions try to find out if the text has gone through several drafts and if the writer has looked critically at all parts of the text and writing process. Poor performance in this part of the process is signalled by a poorly organised and poorly presented text.

- If the teacher has seen previous drafts of the text, does the present one represent an improvement over the previous drafts?
- In what aspects are there improvements? In what aspects are there no real improvements?
- Is the text clear, well organised and well presented?

*Editing*

These questions try to find out if the writer can systematically make corrections and improvements to the text. Poor performance in this part of the process is signalled by the failure to respond to feedback, repeated errors, careless errors, references in the text not in the list of references, and inconsistencies in the list of references.

- Are there signs of self-correction?
- Is the text free of spelling errors, including those that a spellchecker would not find (e.g. *form–from*)?
- Is the text well formatted and consistently formatted?

Table 8.1 provides a similar list of questions that could be used when interviewing a learner about a particular piece of writing.

The idea behind all these questions is that teachers of writing should be able to look at a piece of writing and make judgements about a writer's control of each of the parts of the writing process. The teacher should also be able to give useful feedback to writers about their strengths and weaknesses in relation to these parts, and provide useful suggestions for improvement. This feedback should involve strategy training where, eventually, learners are able to question themselves about each part of the process so that they can prepare for, monitor, and evaluate their own written work and the written work of others.

**Table 8.1** Using Questions to Assess the Writing Process

| Parts of the writing process | Questions |
| --- | --- |
| Goals of the writer | What was your purpose in doing this piece of writing? <br> What is the main message of your piece of writing? |
| Model of the reader | Who were you writing this for? <br> Did you feel that you should write this with a certain tone? <br> Did you have a clear picture of who you were writing this for? <br> How much knowledge does the reader already have of this topic? <br> Did you think about that when you were doing the writing? |
| Gathering ideas | Do you know a lot about this topic? <br> Did you gather information from various sources before doing the writing? What were these sources? <br> Do you find it easy to gather information for your writing? |
| Organising ideas | Did you use sub-headings in your writing? <br> Did you plan these sub-headings before writing or did you think of them as you wrote? <br> Did you think of the reader when deciding how to organise your writing and what to give prominence to? |
| Ideas to text | Once you had the ideas, did you find it easy to write? <br> How long did it take you to write this? Can you write quickly? <br> Do you find it easier to talk about the ideas than to write them? |
| Reviewing | Are you happy with this piece of writing? <br> Can you see strengths and weaknesses in this piece of writing? What are they? Do you think you could still improve this text? <br> Do you usually find one part of the writing process harder than the others? <br> Do you follow a procedure when checking your writing? |
| Editing | Can you use a spellchecker? Did you use it? <br> Can you use a dictionary to get information on how to use a word? <br> Did you do that in this piece of writing? Where? <br> Are you able to correct many of your errors yourself? <br> Do you follow a model when making a list of references? |

# CHAPTER 9

# Topic Types

The purpose of this chapter is to look at one way of analysing the kind of information that occurs in non-fiction texts. The reason for doing this is to provide learners with a strategy for gathering information to write on a particular topic, and a strategy for taking notes from a reading text or a lecture. Using topic types is most suited to learners who are of at least intermediate proficiency. It is particularly suited to learners with academic goals. Topic type activities are well suited to group work.

## The Topic Type Hypothesis

Although texts may differ in the topic they deal with, they may be similar in that they are all based on the same topic type. For example, a recipe for cooking fish curry, a set of instructions for using a cell-phone, a set of directions to a place, and a description of a teaching technique are all examples of the instruction topic type. The instruction topic type includes texts that tell (or instruct) you how to do something. The instruction topic type has the following parts.

- the tools needed
- the materials or ingredients needed
- the steps involved
- the cautions or conditions involved in some of the steps
- the outcome or result of following the steps.

Not all of these parts need to be present (following a set of directions to get to a place does not need tools or ingredients). The only essential one is the steps. Here is an example of a recipe broken into its parts.

*Dumplings*

| | |
|---|---|
| 1 cup self-raising flour | 1 tablespoon of olive oil |
| pinch of salt | milk to mix |

Mix flour and salt together. Add milk and mix to a soft dough. Add olive oil and mix. Roll into balls the size of a golf ball. Place on top of a gently boiling stew. Cook for about 20 minutes without turning and with the lid on.

| **Materials/ingredients** | flour, salt, milk, olive oil |
|---|---|
| **Tools/equipment** | (bowl, mixing spoon, pot of stew) |
| **Steps** | **Conditions** |
| mix flour and salt<br>add milk<br>mix<br>add olive oil<br>mix<br>roll into balls<br>place on top of stew<br>cook | <br><br>to a soft dough<br><br><br>the size of a golf ball<br>gently boiling<br>for about 20 minutes<br>without turning<br>with the lid on |
| **Result** | Dumplings |

The topic type hypothesis says that texts on different topics but which are all of the same topic type will contain the same general kinds of information.

Johns and Davies (1983) described 12 topic types. Some are much more common than others. Table 9.1 is adapted from Johns and Davies and lists the most important topic types and their parts.

**Table 9.1** The Most Useful Topic Types and their Parts

---

**Characteristics**
What are the features of the thing described?
What is the proof that some of these features exist?
What general category does this thing fit into?
What other information is there about this thing?

**Physical structure**
What are the parts?
Where are the parts located?
What are they like?
What do they do?

**Instruction**
What are the steps involved?
What materials and equipment are needed?
What do we need to be careful about at some steps?
What is the result of the steps?
What does this result show?

**Process**
What are the stages involved in the development?
What material is involved at each stage?
Where and when does each stage occur?
How long does each stage last?
What acts at each stage to bring about change?
What is the thing like at each stage?
What happens at each stage?

**State/situation**
Who are the people, etc. involved?
What time and place are involved?
What is the background leading up to the happening?
What happened?
What are the effects of this happening?

**Principle**
What is the law or principle involved?
Under what conditions does the principle apply?
What are some examples of the principle in action?
How can we check to see that the principle is in action?
How can we apply the principle?

*(Continued overleaf)*

**Table 9.1** Continued.

---

**Theory**
    What is the hypothesis?
    What led to this hypothesis?
    How is it tested?
    What are the results of testing?
    What is the significance of the results?

---

## Topic Types and Writing

An important step in the writing process is getting information to write about. As the parts of a topic type are already specified, once the topic type of a writing topic is known or decided, it is relatively easy to see what kinds of information need to be gathered. For example, if the writing topic is to describe how to cut a circle out of a piece of wood, the instruction topic type, then the information that needs to be gathered is as follows.

1. What are the tools that are needed?
2. What materials, e.g. wood, are needed?
3. What steps need to be followed?
4. Is there anything that needs to be given special attention at any of the steps?

Note that using topic types helps in the gathering of information but does not say how the information should be organised nor how it should be expressed. There are several ways of describing the steps. They can be written as imperatives as in a recipe (add two cups of sugar, mix well), or they can be written as declaratives (the butter is then added).

The following skills are needed when using topic types to help gather information for writing.

1. The learners need to be familiar with the few topic types that are relevant to their area of study. They need to know the parts of each of these topic types.
2. The learners need to be able to relate a particular topic to a particular topic type.

Here are some writing topics with their topic type.

| | |
|---|---|
| What is photosynthesis? | Process |
| How do you make a macro in MS-Word? | Instruction |
| How is chocolate made? | Process |
| Describe the baobab tree. | Characteristics |

| | |
|---|---|
| What was the most frightening thing that happened to you? | State/situation |
| What are lemurs? | Characteristics |
| Why can high interest rates lead to inflation? | Theory |
| What are the parts of the eye? | Physical structure |

Table 9.2 relates topic types and types of writing.

## Topic Types and Reading

Knowledge of topic types is useful when predicting the kind of information that will be in a text, when taking notes from a text, and when evaluating the adequacy of a text.

**Table 9.2** Topic Types and Types of Texts

| Topic type | Types of texts |
|---|---|
| What happened? (state/situation) | Letters Newspaper reports Stories Historical accounts Diary reports |
| What is it like? (characteristics, physical structure) | Consumer reports Magazine article Poems Application form Curriculum vitae Letter of recommendation Course outline |
| How do you do it? (instruction) | Recipes Operating instructions Shopping list Help or troubleshooting notes Article for a teachers' journal Methods section of an experimental report |
| What happens to it? (process) | Science texts |
| Why does it happen? (theory, principle) | Science texts |

*Predicting from the Title of a Text*

The teacher tells the learners the title of a text they are going to read. If the learners already know about topic types, they then decide what topic type the text is likely to be. They can then list the questions for each part of the topic type and suggest answers to those questions which are closely related to the topic of the text. If the learners are not familiar with topic types, the teacher tells the learners the relevant topic type and then gives them the general questions for each part of the topic type. The learners work in groups to suggest answers for each question. After they see the text the learners can then comment on the accuracy of their predictions.

Here is an example based on a text called *Limestone caves,* an example of the process topic type.

> What are the stages involved in the development of a limestone cave?
> What material is involved at each stage?
> Where (location) and when does each stage occur?
> How long (time) does each stage last?
> What (instrument) acts on the cave at each stage to bring about change?
> What is the cave like (property or structure) at each stage?
> What happens (action) at each stage?

*Taking Notes from a Text*

After looking quickly at the text, the learners decide what topic type it is. Deciding on the topic type is similar to answering the general question "What am I supposed to learn from this text?". If brief notes are going to be taken, they should possibly focus on the obligatory part of the topic type, for example the steps in an instruction text, or the parts in a physical structure text. If the learner wants to take detailed notes, it may be worth filling in an information transfer diagram based on the parts of the topic type (see Nation and Newton, 2009 for more discussion of information transfer). Here are some examples.

Process

| Stage | Material and structure | Location | Time | Instrument and action |
|-------|------------------------|----------|------|------------------------|
|       |                        |          |      |                        |
|       |                        |          |      |                        |
|       |                        |          |      |                        |
|       |                        |          |      |                        |

Physical Structure

| Parts | Location | Features | Function |
|---|---|---|---|
| | | | |
| | | | |
| | | | |

State/situation

| Who | Where | When |
|---|---|---|

| Background | | Event | | Future effects |
|---|---|---|---|---|
| | $\rightarrow$ | | $\rightarrow$ | |

Detailed note-taking like this may be useful if the learners are eventually going to write about what they have read.

### Evaluating the Adequacy of a Text

The parts of a topic type cover what can be included in a text. However, not all this information is necessarily included in a particular text. There are several reasons for this. First, some of the information may be so well known or obvious that it does not need stating. For example, in a physical structure text describing a flowering plant, there might not be any mention of the location of the roots of the plant because everybody knows that for most plants these are the lowest part of a plant and are under the ground. Second, a part of a topic type may not be mentioned because that piece of information is not seen as being important for the purpose of that text. For example, a description of the digestive process might not include information about what acts at each stage to bring about the change, because the main focus may be on the state of the food which is being digested at each stage rather than the causes of the change of state. Third, a part of a topic type may not be mentioned because the writer did not plan the piece of writing well or because the writer did not consider what the reader needed to know. In this case, checking the text against the parts of the topic type could reveal what is missing and help decide if the missing parts should really be there.

## Limitations of the Topic Type Approach

Topic type analysis works well with texts that have a clear communicative purpose and that use only one or at most two topic types. This present chapter about topic types uses two topic types—characteristics (What are topic types? What are they like?) and instruction (How do you use topic types? What techniques can be used with them?).

The parts of topic types can be at different levels of grammatical analysis. For example, some parts may be nouns or noun groups, while others may be whole sentences or several sentences. In the classification topic type for example, the item being defined and the group it fits into are usually noun groups, while the defining characteristics can be a clause, a whole sentence or several sentences. This is not a serious problem but it makes the use of information transfer diagrams more difficult.

While there has been some work and research on topic types (Johns and Davies, 1983; Nagabhand, Nation and Franken, 1993; Franken, 1987) this has not been enough to truly test and develop the idea, and to expand and refine the list of topic types.

One problem in using topic types for analysis is that in some texts two topic types are used at the same time. One is used to make the text interesting and engaging for the reader, and the other relates to the information that the reader should get from the text (Nagabhand, Nation and Franken, 1993). Here is an example.

### Coconuts

Once, when I was small, I bought a coconut with my pocket money. As I carried it home, I could hear liquid sloshing about inside. I could see three things that looked like eyes, on one end. When I got it home, I wasn't sure what part you were supposed to eat. (Crook, 1978).

In this text, the state/situation topic type (What happened?) is used as a way of making the text interesting and accessible for young readers. However, the content of the text (what learners should get from reading the text) is best viewed as an example of the characteristics topic type which tells what something is like, in this case what coconuts are like. The way to test for this is to ask "What should the learners know after reading this text?". Clearly the answer for the above text is not what happened in the story (state/situation) but what coconuts are like (characteristics).

This leads to the last caution when using topic types. Topic types deal only with the information in a text not with the structure of the discourse nor the vocabulary and grammatical devices used to express the information. It is possible to see connections between topic types and organisation and grammar and vocabulary, but these are not the main focus of a topic type approach.

Perhaps the greatest value of a topic type approach is in gathering ideas for writing where the topic clearly fits into a known topic type. Using guiding questions like those in Table 9.1 or information transfer diagrams can be a very effective way of putting learners in control of the data-gathering part of the writing process (Franken, 1987).

CHAPTER **10**
# Responding to Written Work

The assessment of learners' written work can have a range of goals. These goals can be classified under various headings. First, as we have seen in Chapter 8 on the writing process, assessment can focus on the product or the piece of writing itself, or on the process of writing. Second, assessment can differ in its purposes. It can aim at making a summative judgement on the learners' writing for the purpose of awarding a grade, or passing or failing. It can aim at a formative shaping of the learners' progress in writing by diagnosing problems, by providing encouragement to keep writing and to write more, and by providing constructive feedback on the content and form of the writing. Table 10.1 lists one range of options.

## Motivating

Positive feedback on the content of learners' writing can do a lot to increase the amount of writing that learners do and to improve their attitude to writing. This feedback includes comments like the following.

"The part about the fire was really interesting. Can you tell me more about that?"
"You wrote that the end of the movie surprised you. What were you expecting?"

Written feedback like this tells the writer that their work is being read, is understood, and interests the reader. Especially with younger learners, it is important not to discourage writing by always giving feedback that points

**Table 10.1** Goals, Purpose and Means of Writing Assessment

| Goals | Purpose | Means |
|---|---|---|
| Motivating | Increase amount of writing Develop a love of writing | Positive feedback on the content Publication of the writing |
| Improving the quality of writing | Improve the written product Improve control of the writing process | Peer feedback Conferencing Marking of errors Analytic assessment Use of checklists Self-assessment |
| Diagnosing problems | Finding poorly controlled parts of the writing process | Analysis of the product Observation of the process |
| Measuring proficiency | Award a grade | Holistic assessment Analytic assessment Assessment of a portfolio |

out the errors in the writing. There should be a place in a writing course for feedback on errors but this kind of feedback needs to be very carefully balanced against the positive encouragement to write more, and these two kinds of feedback need to be separated.

Another form of positive feedback is publication. This can take many forms. Reading written work aloud to others is a form of publication. Having your work circulated or posted on the wall of the classroom is another, and having it appear in a printed collection is yet another.

Some learners are embarrassed by praise, especially in the presence of peers. One way of dealing with this is to praise the piece of work not the person. That is, rather than say "You did a good job with the introduction", some learners may find it more acceptable to hear "The introduction was very clear and well organised".

The motivation to write is most helped by learners doing a lot of successful writing. **Speed writing** involves the learners writing for a set time each day and keeping a graph of the number of words written within that fixed time. Special praise is given to those who increase the amount they write within that time.

### Improving the Quality of Writing

In Chapter 8 we have looked at ways of providing feedback on the various parts of the writing process. The techniques used to provide feedback to learners on their writing can differ over a range of factors. Table 10.2 lists the possibilities.

**Table 10.2** Factors Involved in Giving Feedback

---

**Source of feedback**
Teacher
Peers
Self

**Mode of feedback**
Spoken
Written
Both

**Size of audience**
Whole class
Small group
Individual

**Focus of the feedback**
Product—several aspects or narrow focus
Process—several aspects or narrow focus

**Form of the feedback**
Comments
Scale
Checklist

**Amount of writing**
Single piece of writing
A portfolio of writing

---

1. *Source of feedback.* The feedback can come from the teacher, from peers, and from the learners themselves in self-assessment. The use of peer feedback can reduce the teacher's load but is also very valuable in helping writers develop a sense of audience. The use of self-assessment encourages metacognitive awareness of the writing process and the qualities of good writing.

2. *Mode of feedback.* Feedback can be written or spoken or a combination of these. Spoken feedback allows a dialogue to exist between the writer and the source of feedback. It may also be more effective in getting the writer's attention than written feedback. Written feedback provides a lasting record which can be used to measure progress and to act as a reminder.

3. *Size of the audience.* A teacher can give feedback to the whole class, to small groups or to individuals. Where there are common problems in the class, feedback to the whole class can save a lot of time. Working at the individual level, as in conferencing, can provide an opportunity to explore issues as well as give feedback.

4. *Focus of the feedback.* Feedback can focus on aspects of the written product as, for example, when marking scales are used. It can also

focus on the parts of the writing process. The focus can also cover a range of aspects or parts of the process, or it can be narrowed down to focus on only one or two. Having a narrow focus can make peer evaluation more effective.

5. *Form of the feedback.* Feedback can be guided by the use of checklists or scales. Feedback can be uncontrolled when spoken or written comments are given on the strengths and weaknesses of the piece of writing without the systematic coverage of a scale. Upshur and Turner (1995) describe a way of making scales which can be used for marking large quantities of tests with reasonable reliability and validity.

6. *Amount of the writing looked at.* Feedback can be given on parts of a piece of writing, for example, when someone sits next to the writer and reads what they have just written after every two or three sentences are written. Feedback can be given on the whole of a piece of writing, or on a portfolio of writing. The advantages of seeing a portfolio are that a range of genres can be looked at, the learner's progress over time can be seen and commented on, and the assessment is likely to be more reliable and valid because of the numerous points of assessment.

Let us now look at some techniques for providing feedback that draw on the factors we have just considered. The various combinations of these factors provide a very large number of feedback possibilities. We will look at a few that together cover most of the factors.

### Written Feedback to the Class

Where learners in the class have common weaknesses and strengths in their writing, an efficient way of giving feedback is to prepare a written report that is handed out to the class. This report can detail what the best pieces of writing were like, what the common errors and weaknesses were, and what to do about them. The teacher may also make individual written comments on each piece of writing but these need not be so extensive if they are accompanied by a class handout.

This sheet also provides a useful record that can be looked at again by the teacher for later pieces of writing or for other years to see if the strengths and weaknesses are the same or have changed.

If a grade is given to the pieces of writing, the handout sheet can also explain the range of grades and the criteria for each step in the grading scale.

### Oral Feedback to the Whole Class

A very effective way to give feedback on writing is to get the permission of two or three learners to put their pieces of writing on an overhead projector transparency and then go through them orally with the whole class. In effect, the learners are watching the teacher mark a piece of work and this can help the learners see what the teacher is looking for and what the teacher values in a piece of writing. The teacher can also ask the learners to comment and can interact with them on points in the piece of writing. This obviously has to be done tactfully and with praise for the writing playing a large part in the commentary. The name of the writer could be kept confidential, but this is unlikely to be successful in a small class where learners know each other reasonably well.

It is worth remembering that when the good points and bad points are mentioned, it is better to end with the good points so that the writer is left with a positive feeling about the piece of writing. If learners know that everyone has a chance of having their writing discussed in this way, they may be less likely to use it as a way of making fun of others.

*Individual Feedback Using a Scale*

One way of speeding up marking and making sure a balanced range of aspects of writing are dealt with is to mark each learner's work using a scale. Each part of the scale can be accompanied by a brief comment explaining why that point on the scale was chosen. Here is an example of a scale.

| Aspects of writing | Comments |
|---|---|
| **Richness of vocabulary**<br>1 -------- 2 ------- 3 ------- 4 ------- 5 | |
| **Mechanics (spelling, punctuation)**<br>1 -------- 2 ------- 3 ------- 4 ------- 5 | |
| **Grammatical accuracy and complexity**<br>1 -------- 2 ------- 3 ------- 4 ------- 5 | |
| **Organisation and coherence**<br>1 -------- 2 ------- 3 ------- 4 ------- 5 | |
| **Content**<br>1 -------- 2 ------- 3 ------- 4 ------- 5 | |

The use of a standard feedback tool like a scale gives learners feedback on each of the important aspects of their writing, allows them to see improvement or lack of it for each aspect, and makes them aware of the range of aspects that need to be considered while writing and when reflecting on it. It can be a useful preparation for self-assessment.

*Conferencing on a Portfolio*

Conferencing involves a one-to-one meeting between the teacher and the learner to talk about the learner's writing. A portfolio is a collection of several pieces of the learner's writing, some of which may have already been marked and commented on. The major strength of conferencing is that the learner can provide an explanation of what was involved in the pieces of writing, and can seek clarification from the teacher about the teacher's evaluation of them.

Good conferencing is interactive. It should conclude with clear proposals for future improvement of the writing. Learners can prepare for conferencing either by preparing some questions to ask, or by having a sheet provided by the teacher that gives the learner some questions to consider. These questions can focus on what the teacher expects in the writing.

Conferencing on a portfolio allows the opportunity to look at weaknesses and strengths which appear in several pieces of writing and thus deserve comment. It also allows the opportunity to see improvement across several pieces of writing. This improvement can be in the quantity written, the quality of the writing, and quality and range of the content. Conferencing is also used at different stages of a piece of writing so that the learner is helped to improve a particular piece of writing. Conferencing takes a lot of time but its focused one-to-one interaction brings many benefits.

*Marking Grammatical Errors*

Some pieces of writing can be marked for grammatical accuracy, appropriate use of vocabulary, and spelling. This feedback can have the goal of helping learners develop knowledge and strategies for self-correction. Learners at intermediate and advanced levels appreciate such feedback and ask for it, particularly when they have to write reports, memos, and assignments that others will read.

The most effective way of giving this kind of feedback is to have a set of signals that indicate where the error occurs and what kind of error it is. The learners then have to correct their own errors after they have been marked and show their corrections to the teacher. They do not rewrite the piece of writing but make the corrections on the marked piece of writing. This makes the teacher's checking much easier. See Chapter 8 for such a scheme.

If the number of errors per 100 words is calculated and put on a graph, learners can see their improvement on this aspect of writing. When the errors per 100 words is high, around ten or more errors per 100 words, it is easy to make very quick improvement in grammatical accuracy. This is because many of the errors will involve items like subject-verb agreement, article usage, and verb group construction, which are rule-based. Learning the rules and how to check their application brings quick improvement. When learners are making about three errors per 100 words, improvement is very slow because most of the errors are word-based, involving collocation, appropriacy, and grammatical patterns that apply to certain words.

Such feedback is a useful part of a well-balanced writing course, but it must not be the only kind of feedback. Too much of this detailed, negative feedback can discourage learners from writing and from taking risks when writing.

*Peer Evaluation with a Focus*

Peer evaluation involves learners receiving feedback on their writing from each other. It can be done in pairs or in a small group. Each learner brings the draft of a piece of writing, the others read it, and then give helpful comments. In order to make commenting easier, the learners can be told to focus on one or two aspects of the piece of writing, such as organisation, the quality of the argument, or formal aspects such as the use of headings or references. Usually the learners will make oral comments, but written feedback is also possible.

The main advantages of peer evaluation is that learners get feedback from others besides the teacher. It can help them develop a more balanced model of the reader, who they can then think of when they write. Peer feedback also allows those giving feedback to learn from seeing others' pieces of writing and hearing what others say about them. In the academic world, peer review is an important part of the publication process. It has the two goals of obtaining an adequate product as well as providing training for future writing.

A major problem with peer evaluation is that learners may not value the comments of their peers and see them as being far inferior to the teacher's comments (Zhang, 1995). There are several ways of dealing with this. First, peer evaluation can be a step before teacher evaluation. If learners see that peer evaluation can result in an eventual better evaluation by the teacher, peer evaluation will be valued. Second, the quality of peer evaluation can be raised by providing training in evaluation (Min, 2005 and 2006) and by providing written guidelines to use during the evaluation. These written guidelines can be questions to ask or a checklist. Min's (2006) study shows that training learners in doing peer review results in many more comments being incorporated into the revision, peer comments becoming by far the greatest source of revisions, and in better revisions. The training Min used lasted a total of five hours and involved in-class modelling and one-on-one conferencing outside class. It should be possible to develop a more efficient training system. The benefits make it clearly worth doing.

### Self-evaluation with a Checklist

Part of the writing process is checking over what has been written to make improvements. In formal writing, such as the writing of assignments for academic study, this checking can be helped if there is a checklist of things to consider. Here is a possible checklist.

- ☐ Is your main argument clearly stated?
- ☐ Is it presented very early in the writing?
- ☐ Are the supports for this argument clearly signalled?
- ☐ Are there enough sub-headings?
- ☐ If you look only at the sub-headings, do they cover the main ideas in the assignment?
- ☐ Have you checked carefully for spelling and grammar errors?
- ☐ Are all the references in your text also in the list of references?
- ☐ Are your references complete and do they follow a consistent format?
- ☐ Have you kept within the word limits of the assignment?

A step towards self-assessment is pair checking, where learners work in pairs to check each other's assignment together. That is, both learners read the same assignment together.

### Reformulation

Reformulation involves a native speaker rewriting a learner's piece of writing so that the learner can then compare their first attempt with the reformulation. This is a very time-consuming process which places a heavy burden on the native speaker. However, those who support this procedure speak very highly of it.

### Electronic Feedback

If texts are submitted in electronic form, it is possible to provide feedback using the range of word-processing functions. Here we will look at some of those available in the word-processing program, Microsoft Word, but other programs have similar features.

- *Track changes:* by turning on the Track changes function in the Tools menu, any changes the teacher makes to the text are clearly indicated for the learner to see. Additions are highlighted, and deletions are indicated. The learner can decide to accept or reject these changes and continue to improve the text.

- *Comment:* by turning on the Comment function in the Insert menu, the teacher can add helpful suggestions for improving the text or can praise parts of the text.
- *Font colour:* by selecting part of the text, and changing the font colour (go to the Format menu, choose Font, and click the desired colour), the teacher can mark parts of the text that need careful checking or rewriting. Different colours can be used to mark different problems.
- *Hyperlink:* if the learner has a problem with using a particular word, the teacher can make a small concordance (a list of sentences all containing the problem word) using Tom Cobb's website (www.lextutor.ca) or using a downloadable concordancer and link this short concordance using the hyperlink function in the insert menu. Here is an example of a concordance for *explain.*

1. . . . te smoke screen . . . I have nothing to [[explain]]."<quote/ ><p/> <p__>As for debates, Clin . . .
2. . . . the famous and the powerful squirm and [[explain]], charge and countercharge.<p/> <p__>L . . .
3. . . . re he will call a Press conference to [[explain]] his sorry side of this financial mess.< . . .
4. . . . eting. Failure to attend the meeting or [[explain]] inability to attend, the letters said, . . .
5. . . . ited States, State Department officials [[explain]], now is mainly interested in setting u . . .
6. . . . inted with this sport I should perhaps [[explain]] that divi-dend stripping is essentially . . .
7. . . . resentative of Syria called upon her to [[explain]] that his brother would meet her at the . . .
8. . . . a garrulous American egghead tried to [[explain]] the differ-ence between the Senate and t . . .
9. . . . Department officials were inclined to [[explain]] the April sales decline as a reaction f . . .
10. . . . recorder (the "black box"), which could [[explain]] why two engines fell from the plane a . . .
11. . . . to give a performance himself. This may [[explain]] why sometimes his films let personalit . . .
12. . . . term's law clerks in their search to [[explain]] why Justices Anthony Kennedy, David Sou . . .

By looking at several relevant examples, the learner can work out how to correct the error they made when using this word in their writing. All of these types of feedback require the learners to send their writing as a computer file to the teacher, and the teacher responding to it on the computer (see Gaskell and Cobb, 2004 for further description of these activities).

*Balancing the Feedback in a Course*

A teacher of writing needs to look at the range of feedback options and work out a suitable balance for a particular learner or a course. Balancing the feedback involves:

- Considering the teacher's workload. Having some peer assessment and self-assessment can reduce this.
- Considering how the learners can develop their own self-assessment skills. Having the teacher model assessment, watching peers do it, and practising it with the help of checklists can support this.
- Working out the knowledge learners need to improve their writing. Getting feedback on the writing process, developing grammatical knowledge, and gaining awareness of writing conventions can help this.

## Measuring Proficiency in Writing

A good writing test should satisfy the demands of reliability, validity and practicality. One requirement for reliability is that the test should contain a good number of points of assessment. For writing, this means that any assessment based on one piece of writing is not likely to be reliable. Where the assessment is very important, Elley suggests the $2 \times 3$ rule. That is, learners should be assessed on two pieces of writing which are independently graded by three markers, or on three pieces of writing assessed by two markers. If this is not practical, then there should be at least two pieces of writing, with a second marker where the main marker has doubts.

Analytic marking has also been used as a way of increasing the points of assessment. Analytic marking involves having a marking scheme that awards marks for things like richness and appropriateness of vocabulary use, grammatical accuracy, organisation, and overall communicative effectiveness. For each of these categories, marks from 0 to 5 can be awarded. The marks for all the categories can be added up to get a final grade. This contrasts with holistic marking where the marker reads the piece of writing and awards an overall grade for it. In analytic marking each point on each of the categories is arguably a point of assessment. The debate regarding holistic and analytic marking continues. What is clear from the debate is that assessing learners' writing on just one piece of writing is likely to be neither reliable nor valid.

A valid assessment of writing skill needs to consider the range of purposes for which learners write and the degrees of preparation they bring to writing. Some researchers are not happy with seeing a learner's writing skill summed up in one grade. They argue that it is much more informative and helpful to provide a richer description which provides information about the various aspects of the writing process, indicating both strengths and weaknesses.

Practicality is a major issue with the assessment of writing and has encouraged interest in peer feedback and self-assessment. Certainly, for non-native teachers of English, assessing writing can be a major challenge, usually requiring very high levels of language proficiency on the part of the marker. Marking is also very time-consuming, particularly if feedback to the learner on the piece of writing is required. This has encouraged the use of feedback sheets which provide categories for comments.

# Conclusion

This book has described a wide range of techniques and strategies for improving learners' reading and writing skills. These techniques and strategies should not be seen as isolated activities but need to be seen as ways of bringing the four strands of meaning-focused input, meaning-focused output, language-focused learning, and fluency development into practice. In other words, one of the teacher's most important jobs is to plan so that a course provides a properly balanced set of opportunities for learning. Extensive reading is good. Intensive reading provides valuable opportunities for learning. Quick writing helps develop writing fluency. However, all of these activities need to help each other and be present in the course in the proper proportion, so that learners can have an effective range of useful opportunities to learn the language and develop skill in its use.

There are many different ways of bringing the four strands into a course. It is possible for each lesson or unit of work to include each of the four strands in a roughly equal balance. This may be the easiest way of planning a balance, but if lessons are about an hour long, it is unlikely to be very successful because fluency development, for example, requires some sustained attention, and meaning-focused input works best if there are substantial amounts of input. Bringing the four strands into a unit of work which stretches over a week or two weeks is much more feasible. It is also possible to focus reasonably large parts of the course on one or two strands. Regarding fluency development, Brumfit (1985) talks of "a syllabus with holes" where the holes are parts of the course when no new language items are introduced. These provide opportunities for strengthening and becoming fluent with what is already known.

It is also possible to have a less compartmentalised approach where the four strands blend into each other. For example, a course based around themes may begin with meaning-focused input. This then becomes the focus of meaning-focused output with language-focused learning arising from it. Towards the end of the theme, the activities become fluency development because the learners have become very familiar with the material. This more integrated approach to the four strands needs to be monitored to see that there is a rough balance of time between the strands and that each strand truly exists.

The initial motivation for developing the idea of the four strands was to make sure that courses were not dominated by language-focused learning. Three of the four strands are strongly message focused. However, it is not a virtue to go the other way, so that language-focused learning largely disappears from a course, and incidental learning (picking it up as the course goes along) becomes the sole means of learning. This is a danger to be aware of in content-based instruction (Langman, 2003). There is a place for language-focused learning in language courses and there is plenty of evidence, particularly in vocabulary learning, that a course benefits from having a suitable amount of deliberate attention to language features.

This book has looked at the teaching and learning of reading and writing for learners of English as a second or foreign language. It has suggested principles to guide reading and writing courses, and has described a large number of techniques and activities to put these principles into practice. It is worth considering the principles used to guide the teaching of reading and writing in this book, and those described in the companion book, *Teaching ESL/EFL Listening and Speaking*, to see how much the principles for teaching each of the four skills of listening, speaking, reading, and writing are similar to each other. By doing this, it will be seen that teaching a foreign or second language can most effectively be done by applying a rather short list of principles that are largely supported by research. It has been the goal of this book to show the various ways in which these principles can be applied.

# Appendix 1: Spelling and Pronunciation— Points of Correspondence

This is a list of many of the points of correspondence between spelling and pronunciation which occur in the 1,000 most frequent words of English. The list is intended to help learners and teachers who wish to approach the complex relationships between English pronunciation and spelling systematically. It will help learners to work out the pronunciation of many English words from their spelling. It will help teachers who want to give their students pronunciation practice which will also help their reading, or reading practice with some pay-off in pronunciation. It will also help those who wish to prepare teaching material for these purposes. It can also be used to improve spelling.

There are 110 points of correspondence and they have been classified into three groups. Different teaching strategies apply to these three groups at the 1,000-word level. List A contains the major points for teaching and learning. Because they are frequent, they can be learned as rules and used to predict the pronunciations of a large number of English words. List B also contains important features but since they might interfere with the learning of some of the items in List A, they should be postponed, if possible, or not emphasised as teaching points until the corresponding items in List A are well known. Since generally there are no rules to distinguish List B items from List A items, words containing these features will have to be learned individually. List C contains less frequent points of correspondence which need not be major teaching points but nevertheless will be needed in words chosen to exemplify Lists A and B. Since they can be distinguished from List A and B items they need not be postponed and the more the learners are familiar with them the better, though their frequency does not justify a lot of teaching time at this level. There are also other points of correspondence in the 1,000-word list which are so rare that they have not been included in any of these lists.

These three lists are also subdivided into vowel features and consonant features, and then each point of correspondence is listed alphabetically and numbered accordingly. (AV1 = List A, vowel correspondence, number 1 alphabetically; BC3 = List B, consonant correspondence, number 3 alphabetically.)

In these lists the points of correspondence are stated in a brief form. The following symbols and abbreviations are used:

I = initial, M = medial and F = final word position
str. = in a stressed syllable, unstr. = in an unstressed one
C = a consonant letter, V = a vowel letter

Stressed syllables include primary and secondary stressed syllables, typically where full vowels rather than reduced vowels are used.

**Note:** The letters which correspond to the pronunciation are underlined. Letters which are not underlined are environmental features of the correspondence and do not take part in the correspondence, cf. ca = /k/ (in cat) and al = /ɔː/ (in chalk). The phonemic transcription is that of the *Oxford Advanced Learner's Dictionary of Current English* (revised 3rd edition).

### Learning to Use the Rules

1. Break each of the following words into parts and indicate the spelling rule that applies to each part. If a part is not covered by a rule in the lists, write X above the part. Here are three examples.

| AC10 | AV18 | AC2 | CV23 | AC25 | | BC1 | AV13 | AC35 | AV9 | AC19 |
|------|------|-----|------|------|--|-----|------|------|-----|------|
| f | o | c | u | s | | g | i | v | e | n |

| AC2 | AV16 | X |
|-----|------|-----|
| c | o | ugh |

*ask, direct, vocabulary, learning, when, they, be, persuade, high, would, phrases, figures, much, time, read (past tense), have, one, although, daily, the.*

2. Classify the following words into three groups according to the regularity of their spelling.

Very regular     Partly regular     Irregular

*part, ten, write, allow, rule, break, foreign, if, simple, copy, guide, Thai*

## Applying the Rules

1. Make a list of ten words to introduce the *s* = /s/ correspondence. Make sure that other parts of the words are not a source of difficulty.
2. What should be introduced first, *c* = /s/ or *c* = /k/?
3. This is a part of a reading text used with native speakers who are beginning to read. Which words could be dealt with phonically at this very early stage, which could not?

*Too Big* by Materoa Tangaere (Ready to Read, Learning Media, Wellington, 2000)

I am too big for my jeans. I am too big for my T-shirt. I am too big for my shoes. I am too big for my bike. I am too big for my swing. I am too big for my chair. But I am not too big for a hug.

## Spelling to Pronunciation Correspondences

In the following lists, US pronunciations are noted in a separate column where they differ markedly from British pronunciations. Length marks have been used in the US transcriptions although this is not always common practice in the US.

*List A*

Vowels

|  |  | Brit | US |  |  |
|---|---|---|---|---|---|
| AV1 | a̱ | /æ/ |  | I.M.str. | a̱dd ba̱ck |
| AV2 | a̱ | /ə, ɪ/ |  | I.M.F.unstr. | a̱nd huma̱n comma̱ |
| AV3 | a̱CV̱ | /eɪ/ |  | F. and before suffixes, str. | da̱te bra̱vely |
| AV4 | ai̱ | /eɪ/ |  | M.str. | ra̱in |
| AV5 | a̱l | /ɔːl/ | /ɑːl/ | I.M.str. | a̱lso sa̱lt |
|  | a̱ll | /ɔːl/ | /ɑːl/ | M.F.str. | a̱ll sma̱ller ba̱ll |
|  | (a̱l | /ɔː/ | /ɑːl/ | M.str.) | ta̱lk |
| AV6 | a̱r | /ɑː/ | /ɑːr/ | I.M.F.str. | a̱rm da̱rk fa̱r |
| AV7 | a̱y | /eɪ/ |  | M.F. | pla̱yed ma̱y |
| AV8 | e̱ | /e/ |  | I.M.str. | e̱dge pe̱n |

| | | | | | |
|---|---|---|---|---|---|
| AV9 | e̲ | /ə, ɪ/ | | I.M.unstr. | begin problem |
| AV10 | ea | /i:/ | | I.M.F.str. | eat leaf sea |
| AV11 | ee | /i:/ | | M.F.str. | deep see |
| AV12 | er | /ə/ | /ər/ | M.F.unstr. | pattern never |
| AV13 | i̲ | /ɪ/ | | I.M. | in fish |
| AV14 | i̲CV̲ | /aɪ/ | | F. and before suffixes, str. | time writer |
| AV15 | igh | /aɪ/ | | M.F.str. | might high |
| AV16 | o̲ | /ɒ/ | /ɑ:/ | I.M.str. | on song |
| AV17 | o̲ | /ə/ | | I.M.F.unstr. | obey second to |
| AV18 | o̲CV̲ | /əʊ/ | /oʊ/ | F. and before suffixes, str. | bone chosen |
| AV19 | oo | /u:/ | | M.F.str. | moon too |
| AV20 | (or | /ɔ:/ | /ɑ:r/ | M.F.str. | horse for |
| | (ore | /ɔ:/ | | F.str. | more |
| AV21 | ou | /aʊ/ | | I.M.str. | out loud |
| AV22 | ow | /əʊ/ | | I.M.F. | own blown low |
| AV23 | u̲ | /ʌ/ | | I.M. | up run |
| AV24 | (u̲CV̲ | /ju:/ | | I.M.F. | use human |
| | (u̲CV̲ | /u:/ | | M.F. | rule ruler |
| AV25 | y̲ | /ɪ, i:/ | | F.str. (+ M.str. or unstr.) duty system | |

## Consonants

| | | |
|---|---|---|
| AC1 | (b̲ = /b/ | I.M.F. |
| | (b̲b̲ = /b/ | M. |
| AC2 | (c̲a | |
| | (c̲o = /k/ | I.M. |
| | (c̲u | |
| AC3 | (c̲e | |
| | (c̲i = /s/ | I.M. |
| | (c̲y | |
| AC4 | (c̲C = /k/ | I.M. |
| | (c̲k = /k/ | F. |
| | (i̲c̲ = /ɪk/ | F.unstr. |
| AC5 | (c̲h̲ = /tʃ/ | I.M.F. |
| | (t̲c̲h̲ = /tʃ/ | M.F. |
| AC6 | (d̲ = /d/ | I.M.F. |
| | (d̲d̲ = /d/ | M.F. |
| AC7 | -e̲d̲, -d̲ = /ɪd/ | suffix after /t/ and /d/ |
| AC8 | -e̲d̲, -d̲ = /t/ | suffix after other unvoiced sounds |
| AC9 | -e̲d̲, -d̲ = /d/ | suffix after other voiced sounds |

| | | |
|---|---|---|
| AC10 | (f = /f/ | I.M.F. |
| | (ff = /f/ | M. |
| AC11 | (ga | |
| | (go = /g/ | I.M. |
| | (gu | |
| AC12 | (gC = /g/ | I.M. |
| | (gg = /g/ | M.F. |
| | (g = /g/ | F. |
| AC13 | (ge = /dʒ/ | I.M. |
| | (gi = /dʒ/ | I.M. |
| | (dge = /dʒ/ | F. |
| AC14 | h = /h/ | I.M. |
| AC15 | j = /dʒ/ | I.M. |
| | (dj = /dʒ/ | M.) |
| AC16 | k = /k/ | I.M.F. |
| AC17 | (l = /l/ | I.M.F. |
| | (ll = /l/ | M.F. |
| | (Cle = /l/ | F. |
| AC18 | (m = /m/ | I.M.F. |
| | (mm = /m/ | M. |
| AC19 | (n = /n/ | I.M.F. |
| | (nn = /n/ | M. |
| AC20 | (nk | |
| | (n.g = /ŋ/ | M. before /k/ or /g/ |
| AC21 | ng = /ŋ/ | M.F. |
| AC22 | (p = /p/ | I.M.F. |
| | (pp = /p/ | M. |
| AC23 | qu = /kw/ | I.M. |
| AC24 | (r = /r/ | I.M. after C or between Vs |
| | (rr = /r/ | M. |
| AC25 | (s = /s/ | I. in grammatical and lexical words, F. in lexical words only |
| | (ss = /s/ | M.F. |
| | (sC = /s/ | M.F. when the C is unvoices |
| AC26 | (Vse = /z/ | F. |
| | (VsV = /z/ | M. |
| AC27 | -es, -s, -=s = /iz/ | suffixes after /s/, /z/, /ʃ/, /ʒ/, /tʃ/ and /dʒ/ |
| AC28 | -s, -=s = /s/ | suffixes after other unvoiced sounds |
| AC29 | -s, -=s = /z/ | suffixes after other voiced sounds |
| AC30 | sh = /ʃ/ | I.M.F. |
| AC31 | (t = /t/ | I.M.F. |
| | (tt = /t/ | M. |
| AC32 | th = /θ/ | I.F. in lexical words |

| AC33 | t͟h = /ð/ | I. in grammatical words, M. in common lexical and grammatical words |
|---|---|---|
| AC34 | t͟io͟n = /ʃn/ | F. and before suffixes, unstr. |
| AC35 | v͟ = /v/ | I.M. |
| AC36 | w͟ = /w/ | I.M. when first letter in a syllable or following a C |
| AC37 | w͟h͟ = /hw/, /w/ | I. |
| AC38 | (x͟ = /ks/ | M. and F. after a stressed vowel |
|  | (x͟C = /ks/ | M. |
| AC39 | y͟ = /j/ | I. and M. when y͟ is the first letter in a syllable |
| AC40 | z͟ = /z/ | I.M.F. |

*List B*

Vowels

| | | Brit | US | | |
|---|---|---|---|---|---|
| BV1 | a͟ | /ɑ:/ | /æ/ | I.M.str. | a͟sk gla͟ss |
| BV2 | (wa͟ | | | | |
| | (wha͟ | /ɒ/ | | M.str. | wa͟nt wha͟t qua͟rrel |
| | (qua͟ | | | | |
| | ((wa͟r | | | | |
| | (qua͟r | /ɔ:/ | /ɔ:r/ | M.F.str. | wa͟rm qua͟rter) |
| BV3 | ea͟ | /e/ | | M.str. | brea͟d |
| BV4 | o͟ | /ʌ/ | | I.M.str. | o͟ther so͟n |
| BV5 | oo͟ | /ʊ/ | | M.str. | boo͟k |
| BV6 | ow͟ | /aʊ/ | | M.F.str. | tow͟n cow͟ |
| BV7 | (V͟me a | /æ/ | | | |
| | (V͟ne i | /ɪ/ | | | |
| | (V͟ve o | /ɒ/ | /ɑ:/ | | ha͟ve͟ gi͟ve͟ go͟ne͟ |
| | | | | | do͟ne͟ |
| | ( o | /ʌ/ | | | |

Consonants

| BC1 | (ge͟ | | get forget |
|---|---|---|---|
| | (gi͟ = /g/ | I.M. | girl begin |
| BC2 | w͟ho = /h/ | I. | w͟hole |
| BC3 | x͟ = /gz/ | M. before a stressed vowel | ex͟ample |

*List C*

Vowels

| | | Brit | US | | |
|---|---|---|---|---|---|
| CV1 | ai | /ɪ/ | | M.unstr. | capt<u>ai</u>n |
| CV2 | air | /eə/ | /eər/ | F. and before suffixes, str. | h<u>air</u> unf<u>air</u>ly |
| CV3 | ar | /ə/ | /ər/ | F. and before suffixes, unstr. | sug<u>ar</u> regul<u>ar</u>ly |
| CV4 | are | /eə/ | /eər/ | M.F.str. | sh<u>are</u>s c<u>are</u> |
| CV5 | aw | /ɔː/ | /ɑː/ | M.F.str. | dr<u>aw</u>n l<u>aw</u> |
| CV6 | -day | /ɪ/ | /eɪ/ | F. in unstr. suffixes | holi<u>day</u> |
| CV7 | eCV | /iː/ | | F.str. | th<u>ese</u> |
| CV8 | ear | /ɪə/ | /ɪər/ | F.str. | y<u>ear</u> |
| CV9 | ear | /ɜː/ | /ɜːr/ | I.M.str. | <u>ear</u>n h<u>ear</u>d |
| CV10 | ew | /juː, uː/ | | M.F.str. | n<u>ew</u>s f<u>ew</u> |
| CV11 | ey | /ɪ/ | | F.unstr. | mon<u>ey</u> |
| CV12 | ie | /ɪ/ | | in -ied suffixes, unstr. | cop<u>ie</u>d |
| CV13 | ie | /iː/ | | M.str. | p<u>ie</u>ce |
| CV14 | ie | /aɪ/ | | F. and before suffixes, str. | d<u>ie</u> tr<u>ie</u>d |
| CV15 | ir | /ɜː/ | /ɜːr/ | M.str. | b<u>ir</u>d |
| CV16 | o | /əʊ/ | /oʊ/ | F. and before suffixes, str. | s<u>o</u> g<u>o</u>es |
| CV17 | oa | /əʊ/ | /oʊ/ | M.str. | r<u>oa</u>d |
| CV18 | oi | /]ɪ/ | | I.M.str. | <u>oi</u>l v<u>oi</u>ce |
| CV19 | or | /ə/ | /ər/ | M. before consonants, F.unstr. | eff<u>or</u>t doct<u>or</u> |
| CV20 | ou | /ə/ | | M.unstr. | fam<u>ou</u>s |
| CV21 | our | /ə/ | | F.unstr. | col<u>our</u> (not in US) |
| CV22 | oy | /ɔɪ/ | | F.str. | b<u>oy</u> |
| CV23 | u | /ə/ | | M.unstr. | s<u>u</u>ccess |
| CV24 | ue | /uː/ | | F. and before suffixes | bl<u>ue</u> arg<u>ue</u>d |
| CV25 | ur | /ɜː/ | /ɜːr/ | M.str. | b<u>ur</u>n |
| CV26 | ur | /ə/ | /ər/ | M.unstr. | s<u>ur</u>prise |
| CV27 | ure | /ʊə/ | /ʊər/ | | |
| | | /jʊə/ | /jʊər/ | F.str. | p<u>ure</u> |
| CV28 | ure | /ə/ | /ər/ | F.unstr. | pict<u>ure</u> |
| CV29 | y | /aɪ/ | | F.str. | dr<u>y</u> |

Consonants

| | | | |
|---|---|---|---|
| CC1 | k<u>n</u> = /n/ | I. | <u>kn</u>ow |
| CC2 | <u>ph</u> = /f/ | I.M.F. | <u>ph</u>otogra<u>ph</u> |
| | | | tele<u>ph</u>one |
| CC3 | C<u>se</u> = /s/ | F. | hor<u>se</u> |
| CC4 | <u>s</u>C = /z/ | M. before a voiced C | hu<u>s</u>band |
| CC5 | <u>s</u> = /z/ | F. in grammatical words | i<u>s</u> |
| CC6 | <u>wr</u> = /r/ | I. | <u>wr</u>ite |

## Pronunciation to Spelling Correspondences

Vowels

/ɑ:/     = <u>ar</u> (AV6); <u>a</u> (BV1)
/æ/     = <u>a</u> (AV1); <u>a</u>Ce (BV7)
/aɪ/     = <u>i</u>CV (AV14); <u>igh</u> (AV15); <u>ie</u> (CV14); <u>y</u> (CV29)
/aʊ/     = <u>ou</u> (AV21); <u>ow</u> (BV6)
/e/     = <u>e</u> (AV8); <u>ea</u> (BV3)
/ə/     = <u>a</u> (AV2); <u>e</u> (AV9); <u>er</u> (AV12); <u>o</u> (AV17); <u>ar</u> (CV3); <u>or</u> (CV19); <u>ou</u> (CV20); <u>our</u> (CV21); <u>u</u> (CV23); <u>ur</u> (CV26); <u>ure</u> (CV28)
/ɜ:/     = <u>ear</u> (CV9); <u>ir</u> (CV15); <u>ur</u> (CV25)
/eə/     = <u>air</u> (CV2); <u>are</u> (CV4)
/eɪ/     = <u>a</u>CV (AV3); <u>ai</u> (AV4); <u>ay</u> (AV7)
/əʊ/     = <u>o</u>CV (AV18); <u>ow</u> (AV22); <u>o</u> (CV16); <u>oa</u> (CV17)
/i:/     = <u>ea</u> (AV10); <u>ee</u> (AV11); <u>e</u>CV (CV7); <u>ie</u> (CV13)
/ɪ/     = <u>a</u> (AV2); <u>e</u> (AV9); <u>I</u> (AV13); <u>y</u> (AV25); <u>i</u>Ce (BV7); <u>ai</u> (CV1); <u>ay</u> (CV6); <u>ey</u> (CV11); <u>ie</u> (CV12)
/ɪə/     = <u>ear</u> (CV8)
/ɒ/     = <u>o</u> (AV16); <u>a</u> (BV2); <u>o</u>Ce (BV7)
/ɔ:/     = <u>al</u> (AV5)
/ɔɪ/     = <u>oi</u> (CV18); <u>oy</u> (CV22)
/ɔ:l/     = <u>al</u>, <u>all</u> (AV5)
/u:/     = <u>oo</u> (AV19); <u>u</u>CV (AV24); <u>ew</u> (CV10); <u>ue</u> (CV24)
/ju:/     = <u>u</u>CV (AV24); <u>ew</u> (CV10)
/ʊ/     = <u>oo</u> (BV5)
/ʊə/     = <u>ure</u> (CV27)
/jʊə/     = <u>ure</u> (CV27)
/ʌ/     = <u>u</u> (AV23); <u>o</u> (BV4); <u>o</u>Ce (BV7)

Consonants

/b/     = <u>b</u>, <u>bb</u> (AC1)
/d/     = <u>d</u>, <u>dd</u> (AC6); -<u>d</u>, -<u>ed</u> (AC7)

/dʒ/   = ge, gi, dge (AC13); j (AC15)
/ɪd/   = -d, -ed (AC7)
/f/   = f, ff (AC10); ph (CC2)
/g/   = ga, go, gu (AC11); gC, gg, g (AC12); ge, gi (BC1)
/gs/   = x (BC3)
/h/   = h (AC14); wh (BC2)
/hw/   = wh (AC37)
/j/   = y (AC39)
/k/   = ca, co, cu (AC2); cC, ck (AC4); k (AC16)
/ks/   = x, xC (AC38)
/kw/   = qu (AC23)
/ɪk/   = ic (AC4)
/l/   = l, ll, Cle (AC17)
/m/   = m, mm (AC18)
/n/   = n, nn (AC19); kn (CC1)
/ŋ/   = nc, nk, n.g (AC20); ng (AC21)
/p/   = p, pp (AC22)
/r/   = r, rr (AC24); wr (CC6)
/s/   = ce, cl, cy (AC3); s, ss, sC (AC25); -s, -=s (AC28)
/ʃ/   = sh (AC30)
/ʃn/   = tion (AC34)
/t/   = -ed, -d (AC7); t, tt (AC31)
/tʃ/   = ch, tch (AC5)
/θ/   = th (AC32)
/ð/   = th (AC33)
/v/   = v, ve (AC35)
/w/   = w (AC36); wh (AC37)
/z/   - Vse, VsV (AC25); -s, -es, -=s (AC29); z (AC40); zC (CC4); s
        (CC5)

(This list was developed by R. L. Fountain and revised by C. McGhie)

*References*

Albrow, K. 1972. *The English Writing System: Notes Towards a Description*. London: Longman.
Carney, E. 1997. *English Spelling*. New York: Routledge.
Venezky, R. L. 1970. *The Structure of English Orthography*. The Hague: Mouton.
Wijk, A. 1966. *Rules for the Pronunciation of English*. London: Oxford University Press.

# Appendix 2: A List of Conjunction Relationships

| Relationship | Markers | Meaning | Weighting |
|---|---|---|---|
| 1. Inclusion | and, furthermore, besides, also, similarly, in addition | A and B should be considered together | AB = |
| 2. Alternative | or, nor, alternatively | A and B represent alternatives | AB = |
| 3. Time; arrangement | when, before, after, subsequently, while, then, firstly, finally | A and B actually occurred in this time or sequence relationship, or A and B are arranged in this sequence by the writer | AB = |
| 4. Explanation | in other words, that is to say, I mean, namely | B restates or explains A | AB = |

| Relationship | Markers | Meaning | Weighting |
|---|---|---|---|
| 5. Amplification | to be more specific, thus, therefore, consists of, can be divided into | B describes A in more detail | A |
| 6. Exemplification | for example, such as, thus, for instance | B is an example of A | A |
| 7. Summary, conclusion | to sum up, in short, in a word, to put it briefly | B summarises A | B |
| 8. Cause–effect | because, since thus, as a result, so that, in order to | A is the cause or reason for B | B |
| 9. Contrast | but, although, despite, yet, however, still, on the other hand, nevertheless | B is contrary to the expectation raised by A | B |
| 10. Exclusion | instead, rather than, on the contrary | B excludes A | B |

# References

Allen, J.P.B. and Pit Corder, S. (eds) 1974. *Techniques in Applied Linguistics: Edinburgh Course in Applied Linguistics Vol. 3.* London: Oxford University Press.

Anderson, J. 1971. Selecting a suitable reader: procedures for teachers to assess language difficulty. *RELC Journal* 2, 2: 35–42.

Arndt, V. 1987. Six writers in search of texts: a protocol-based study of L1 and L2 writing. *ELT Journal* 41, 4: 257–267.

Ashton-Warner, S. 1963. *Teacher.* New York: Simon and Schuster.

Bamford, J. and Day, R.R. (eds) 2004. *Extensive Reading Activities for Teaching Language.* Cambridge: Cambridge University Press.

Biber, D. 1989. A typology of English texts. *Linguistics* 27: 3–43.

Biber, D., Johansson, S., Leech, G., Conrad, S. and Finegan, E. 1999. *The Longman Grammar of Spoken and Written English.* New York: Longman.

Bismoko, J. and Nation, I.S.P. 1974. English reading speed and the mother-tongue or national language. *RELC Journal* 5, 1: 86–89.

Bloom, B. (ed.) 1956. *Taxonomy of Educational Objectives. Book 1: Cognitive Domain.* New York: Longmans, Green.

Bradley, L. and Huxford, L. 1994. Organizing sound and letter patterns for spelling. In G.D.A. Brown and N.C. Ellis. Ch. 2: 425–439.

Brown, G.D.A. and Ellis, N.C. 1994. *A Handbook of Spelling.* Chichester: J. Wiley.

Brown, J.D. 1980. Relative merits of four methods of scoring cloze tests. *Modern Language Journal* 64, 3: 311–317.

Brown, J.D. 1997. An EFL readability index. *University of Hawai'i Working Papers in ESL* 15, 2: 85–119.

Bruce, D. 1964. An analysis of word sounds by young children. *British Journal of Educational Psychology* 34: 158–170.

Brumfit, C.J. 1985. Accuracy and fluency: a fundamental distinction for communicative teaching methodology. In C.J. Brumfit, *Language and literature teaching: From practice to principle.* Oxford: Pergamon.

Carver, R.P. 1994. Percentage of unknown vocabulary words in text as a function of the relative difficulty of the text: implications for instruction. *Journal of Reading Behavior* 26, 4: 413–437.

Carver, R.P. 1982. Optimal rate of reading prose. *Reading Research Quarterly* 18: 56–88.

Chambers, F. 1985. Writing: a medical approach. *Modern English Teacher* 12, 4: 38–39.

Chambers, F. and Brigham, A. 1989. Summary writing: a short cut to success. *English Teaching Forum* 27, 1: 43–45.

Chung, H. 1995. Effects of elaborative modification on second language reading comprehension and incidental vocabulary learning. *University of Hawai'i Working Papers in ESL* 14, 1: 27–61.

Chung, M. and Nation, I.S.P. 2006. The effect of a speed reading course. *English Teaching* 61, 4: 181–204.

Cobb, T. 1997. Is there any measurable learning from hands-on concordancing? *System* 25, 3: 301–315.

Cobb, T., Greaves, C. and Horst, M. 2001. Can the rate of lexical acquisition from reading be increased? An experiment in reading French with a suite of on-line resources. In P. Raymond and C. Cornaire, *Regards sur la didactique des langues secondes*. Montréal: Éditions logique: 133–153.

Cramer, S. 1975. Increasing reading speed in English or in the national language. *RELC Journal* 6, 2: 19–23.

Crook, G. 1978. Coconuts. *School Journal* 2, 2: 9–16.

Cunningham, A. and Stanovich, K. 1991. Tracking the unique effects of print exposure in children: associations with vocabulary, general knowledge and spelling. *Journal of Educational Psychology* 83, 2: 264–274.

Davies, A. and Widdowson, H.G. 1974. Reading and writing. In J.P.B. Allen and S. Pit Corder 1974: 155–177.

Day, R.R. and Bamford, J. 1998. *Extensive Reading in the Second Language Classroom.* Cambridge: Cambridge University Press.

Day, R. and Park, J. 2005. Developing reading comprehension. *Reading in a Foreign Language* 17, 1: 60–73.

Dixon, D. 1986. Teaching composition to large classes. *English Teaching Forum* 24, 3: 2–5, 10.

Dowhower, S.L. 1989. Repeated reading: Research into practice. *The Reading Teacher* 42: 502–507.

Dykstra, G. 1964. Eliciting language practice in writing. *ELT Journal* 19, 1: 23–26.

Dykstra, G. and Paulston, C.B. 1967. Guided composition. *ELT Journal* 21, 2: 136–141.

Dykstra, G., Port, R. and Port, A. 1966. *Ananse Tales.* New York: Teachers College Press, Columbia University.

Edge, J. 1985. Do TEFL articles solve problems? *ELT Journal* 39, 3: 153–157.

Ehri, L., Nunes, S., Willows, D., Schuster, B.V., Yaghoub-Zadeh, Z. and Shanahan, T. 2001. Phonemic awareness instruction helps children learn to read: Evidence from the National Reading Panel's meta-analysis. *Reading Research Quarterly* 36, 3: 250–289.

Elgort, I. 2007. *The role of intentional decontextualised learning in second language vocabulary acquisition.* PhD Thesis, Victoria University of Wellington, New Zealand.

Elley, W.B. 1991. Acquiring literacy in a second language: the effect of book-based programs. *Language Learning* 41, 3: 375–411.

Elley, W.B. and Mangubhai, F. 1981a. *The Impact of a Book Flood in Fiji Primary Schools.* Wellington: NZCER.

Elley, W.B. and Mangubhai, F. 1981b. The long-term effects of a book flood on children's language growth. *Directions* 7: 15–24.

Forrester, J. 1968. *Teaching Without Lecturing.* Bombay: Oxford University Press.

Franken, M. 1987. Self-questioning scales for improving academic writing. *Guidelines* 9, 1: 1–8.

Franken, M. 1988. *Topic type as input to an academic topic.* Unpublished M.A. Thesis, Victoria University of Wellington.

Fry, E. 1965. *Teaching Faster Reading: A Manual.* Cambridge: Cambridge University Press.

Fry, E. 1967. *Reading Faster: A Drill Book.* Cambridge: Cambridge University Press.

Gaskell, D. and Cobb, T. 2004. Can learners use concordance feedback for writing errors? *System* 32, 3: 301–319.

George, H.V. 1963. A verb form frequency count. *ELT Journal* 18, 1: 31–37.

George, H.V. 1965. The substitution table. *ELT Journal* 20, 1: 46–48.

George, H.V. 1972. *Common Errors in Language Learning.* Rowley, Mass.: Newbury House.

Glynn, T., Crooks, T., Bethune, N., Ballard, K. and Smith, J. 1989. *Reading Recovery in Context.* Wellington: Dept of Education.

Grabe, W. and Kaplan, R.B. 1996. *Theory and Practice of Writing.* Harlow: Addison, Wesley Longman.

Griffin, S. 1992. Reading aloud: an educator comments . . . *TESOL Quarterly* 26, 4: 784–787.

Guthrie, J.R. 2003. Concept-oriented reading instruction. In A. Sweet and C. Snow (eds) *Rethinking reading comprehension.* New York: Guilford Press: 115–140.

Guthrie, J., Wigfield, A. and Barbosa, P. 2002. http://www.cori.umd.edu/Research/Papers/ IncrRead.htm.

Guthrie, J., Wigfield, A. and Von Secker, C. 2000. Effects of integrated instruction on motivation and strategy use in reading. *Journal of Educational Psychology* 92, 2: 331–341.

Halliday, M.A.K. and Hasan, R. 1976. *Cohesion in English.* London: Longmans.

Henry, R. 1984. Reader generated questions: a tool for improving reading comprehension. *TESOL Newsletter* 18, 3: 29.

Hill, D.R. 1997. Survey review: graded readers. *ELT Journal* 51, 1: 57–81.

Hill, D.R. 2001. Graded readers. *ELT Journal* 55, 3: 300–324.

Hill, D.R. and Thomas, H.R. 1988a. Survey review: graded readers (Part 1). *ELT Journal* 42, 1: 44–52.

Hill, D.R. and Thomas, H.R. 1988b. Survey review: graded readers (Part 2). *ELT Journal* 42, 2: 124–136.

Hill, D.R. and Thomas, H.R. 1989. Seven series of graded readers. *ELT Journal* 43, 3: 221–231.

Hill, L.A. 1966. *Free Composition Book.* London: Oxford University Press.

Hill, L.A. 1969. Delayed copying. *ELT Journal* 23, 3: 238–239.

Hillocks, G. 1984. What works in teaching composition: a meta-analysis of experimental treatment studies. *American Journal of Education* 93, 1: 133–171.

Hillocks, G. 1991. *Research on Written Composition: New Directions for Teaching.* ERIC/NCTE, Urbana-Champaign.

Hirsh, D. and Nation, P. 1992. What vocabulary size is needed to read unsimplified texts for pleasure? *Reading in a Foreign Language* 8, 2: 689–696.

Hu, M. and Nation, I.S.P. 2000. Unknown vocabulary density and reading comprehension. *Reading in a Foreign Language* 13, 1: 403–430.

Hulstijn, J.H. 1993. When do foreign-language readers look up the meaning of unfamiliar words? The influence of task and learner variables. *Modern Language Journal* 77, 2: 139–147.

Ilson, R. 1962. The dicto-comp: a specialized technique for controlling speech and writing in Language Learning. *Language Learning* 12, 4: 299–301.

Iwano, M. 2004. One-minute reading. In R.R. Day and J. Bamford (eds): 86–87.

Jacobs, G. 1986. Quickwriting: a technique for invention in writing. *ELT Journal* 40, 4: 282–290.

Janzen, J. and Stoller, F. 1998. Integrating strategic reading in L2 instruction. *Reading in a Foreign Language* 12, 1: 251–269.

Johns, T. and Davies, F. 1983. Text as a vehicle for information: the classroom use of written texts in teaching reading as a foreign language. *Reading in a Foreign Language* 1, 1: 1–19.

Kim, Y. 2006. Effects of input elaboration on vocabulary acquisition through reading by Korean learners of English as a foreign language. *TESOL Quarterly* 40, 2: 341–373.

Knight, S.M. 1994. Dictionary use while reading: The effects on comprehension and vocabulary acquisition for students of different verbal abilities. *Modern Language Journal* 78, 3: 285–299.

Krashen, S.D. 1981. The "fundamental pedagogical principle" in second language teaching. *Studia Linguistica* 35, 1–2: 50–70.

Kraus-Srebrić, E., Brakus, L. and Kentrič, D. 1981. A six-tier cake: an experiment with self-selected learning tasks. *ELT Journal* 36, 1: 19–23.

Langman, J. 2003. The effects of ESL-trained content-area teachers: reducing middle-school students to incidental language learners. *Prospect* 18, 1: 14–26.

Leibman-Kleine, J. 1987. Teaching and researching invention: using ethnography in ESL writing classes. *ELT Journal* 41, 2: 104–111.

Lennon, P. 1990. Investigating fluency in EFL: a quantitative approach. *Language Learning* 40: 387–417.

Mackay, R. and Mountford, A. 1976. Pedagogic alternatives to "explication de texte" as a procedure for teaching reading comprehension with special reference to EST. *Bulletin Pédagogique* 44: 7–21.

McDonough, J. 1985. Academic writing practice. *ELT Journal* 39, 4: 244–247.

Millett, S. 2005. *New Zealand Speed Readings for ESL Learners.* Books 1 and 2. English Language Institute occasional publications 19 and 20. Victoria University of Wellington, New Zealand.

Min, H. 2005. Training students to become successful peer reviewers. *System* 33, 2: 293–308.

Min, H. 2006. The effects of trained peer review on EFL teachers' revision types and writing quality. *Journal of Second Language Writing* 15: 118–141.

Mitchell, J.M. 1953–54. The reproduction exercise. *ELT Journal* 8, 2: 59–63.

Moorman, G., Blanton, W. and McLaughlin, T. 1994. The rhetoric of whole language. *Reading Research Quarterly* 29, 4: 309–332.

Munby, J. 1968. *Read and Think.* London: Longman.

Murdoch, G.S. 1986. A more integrated approach to the teaching of reading. *English Teaching Forum* 24, 1: 9–15.

Nagabhand, S., Nation, P. and Franken, M. 1993. Can text be too friendly? *Reading in a Foreign Language* 9, 2: 895–907.

Nation, I.S.P. 1978. "What is it?" a multipurpose language teaching technique. *English Teaching Forum* 16, 3: 20–23, 32.

Nation, P. 1989. Improving speaking fluency. *System* 17, 3: 377–384.

Nation, I.S.P. 1990. *Teaching and Learning Vocabulary.* New York: Heinle and Heinle.

Nation, I.S.P. 1991. Dictation, dicto-comp and related techniques. *English Teaching Forum* 29, 4: 12–14.

Nation, I.S.P. 1993. Predicting the content of texts. *The TESOLANZ Journal* 1: 37–46.

Nation, I.S.P. 2001. *Learning Vocabulary in Another Language.* Cambridge: Cambridge University Press.

Nation, I.S.P. 2004a. Vocabulary learning and intensive reading. *EA Journal* 21, 2: 20–29.

Nation, I.S.P. 2004b. *Vocabulary Resource Booklet.* ELI Occasional Publication 21. Wellington: School of Linguistics and Applied Language Studies, Victoria University of Wellington, New Zealand. (studentnotes@vicbooks.co.nz) Freely downloadable from http://www.vuw.ac.nz/lals/staff/paul-nation/nation.aspx.

Nation, I.S.P. 2006. How large a vocabulary is needed for reading and listening? *Canadian Modern Language Review* 63, 1: 59–82.

Nation, I.S.P 2008. *Teaching Vocabulary: Strategies and Techniques.* Boston: Heinle Cengage Learning.

Nation, I.S.P. and Beglar, D. 2007 A vocabulary size test. *The Language Teacher* 31, 7: 9–13.

Nation, I.S.P. and Deweerdt, J-P. 2001. A defence of simplification. *Prospect* 16, 3: 55–67.

Nation, I.S.P. and Gu, P.Y. 2007. *Focus on Vocabulary.* Sydney: Macquarie University/NCELTR.

Nation, I.S.P. and Malarcher, C. 2007. *Reading for Speed and Fluency.* Books 1–4. Seoul: Compass Publishing.

Nation, I.S.P. and Newton, J. 2009. *Teaching ESL/EFL Listening and Speaking.* New York: Routledge

Nation, I.S.P. and Soulliere, E. 1991. (eds) *Speed reading and stories from around the world.* Wellington: School of Linguistics and Applied Language Studies, Victoria University of Wellington, New Zealand. (studentnotes@vicbooks.co.nz)

Nation, P. and Wang, K. 1999. Graded readers and vocabulary. *Reading in a Foreign Language* 12, 2: 355–380.

Oller, J.W. 1979. *Language Tests at School.* London: Longman.

Palincsar, A.S. and Brown, A.L. 1986. Interactive teaching to promote independent learning from text. *Reading Teacher* 20: 771–776.

Palmer, D.M. 1982. Information transfer for listening and reading. *English Teaching Forum* 20, 1: 29–33.

Parker, K. and Chaudron, C. 1987. The effects of linguistic simplifications and elaborative modifications on L2 comprehension. *University of Hawai'i Working Papers in ESL* 6, 2: 107–133.

Pica, T. 1986. An interactional approach to the teaching of writing. *English Teaching Forum* 24, 3: 6–10.

Pinker, S. 1999. *Words and Rules. The ingredients of language.* New York: Basic Books.

Purves, A.C., Sofer, A., Takala, S. and Vahapassi, A. 1984. Towards a domain-referenced system for classifying composition assignments. *Research in the Teaching of English* 18, 4: 385–416.

Quinn, E. and Nation, I.S.P. 1974. *Speed Reading.* Kuala Lumpur: Oxford University Press.

Quinn, E., Nation, I.S.P. and Millett, S. 2007. *Asian and Pacific Speed Readings for ESL Learners.* (available from studentnotes@vicbooks.co.nz)

Radford, W.L. 1969. The blackboard composition. *ELT Journal* 24, 1: 49–54.

Radice, F.W. 1978. Using the cloze procedure as a teaching technique. *ELT Journal* 32, 3: 201–204.

Raimes, A. 1985. What unskilled ESL students do as they write: a classroom study of composing. *TESOL Quarterly* 19, 2: 229–258.

Rasinski, T.V. 1990. Effects of repeated reading and listening-while-reading on reading fluency. *Journal of Educational Research* 83, 3: 147–150.

Rasinski, T. and Hoffman, J. 2003. Oral reading in the school literacy curriculum. *Reading Research Quarterly* 38, 4: 510–522.

Rayner, K. 1998. Eye movements in reading and information processing: 20 years of research. *Psychological Bulletin* 124, 3: 372–422.

Riley, P.M. 1972. The dicto-comp. *English Teaching Forum* 10, 1: 21–23.

Rinvolucri, M. 1981. Words—How to teach them. *Modern English Teacher* 9, 2: 19–20.

Rinvolucri, M. 1983. Writing to your students. *ELT Journal* 37, 1: 16–21.

Robinson, P. 1987. Projection into dialogue as composition strategy. *ELT Journal* 41, 1: 30–36.

Rounds, P. 1992. Reading aloud: another educator comments. *TESOL Quarterly* 26, 4: 787–790.

Rye, J. 1985. Are cloze items sensitive to constraints across sentences? A review. *Journal of Research in Reading (UKRA)* 8: 94–105.

Samuels, S.J. 1979. The method of repeated reading. *The Reading Teacher* 32, 4: 403–408.

Saragi, T., Nation, I.S.P. and Meister, G. 1978. Vocabulary learning and reading. *System* 6, 2: 72–78.

Schmidt, R. 1992. Psychological mechanisms underlying second language fluency. *Studies in Second Language Acquisition* 14: 357–385.

Schmitt, N., Schmitt, D. and Clapham, C. 2001. Developing and exploring the behaviour of two new versions of the Vocabulary Levels Test. *Language Testing* 18, 1: 55–88.

Scott, M., Carioni, L., Zanatta, M., Bayer, E. and Quintanilha, T. 1984. Using a "standard exercise" in teaching reading comprehension. *ELT Journal* 38, 2: 114–120.

Simcock, M. 1993. Developing productive vocabulary using the ask and answer technique. *Guidelines* 15: 1–7.

Sindelar, P., Monda, L. and O'Shea, L. 1990. Effects of repeated readings on instructional and mastery level readers. *Journal of Educational Research* 83, 4: 220–226.

Smith, J. and Elley, W. 1997. *How Children Learn to Read.* Auckland: Addison Wesley Longman.

Smith, J. and Elley, W. 2000. *How Children Learn to Write.* Auckland: Addison Wesley Longman.

Spack, R. 1984. Invention strategies and the ESL composition student. *TESOL Quarterly* 18, 4: 649–670.

Spack, R. 1985. Literature, reading, writing and ESL: bridging the gaps. *TESOL Quarterly* 19: 703–725.

Stahl, S., Duffy-Hester, A. and Stahl, K. 1998. Everything you wanted to know about phonics (but were afraid to ask). *Reading Research Quarterly* 33, 3: 338–355.

Stevick, E. 1959. "Technemes" and the rhythm of class activity. *Language Learning* 9, 3 and 4: 45–51.

Strong, W. 1976. Sentence combining: back to basics and beyond. *English Journal* 65, 2: 56, 60–64.

Sweeting, A.E. 1967. *Situational Composition*. Oxford: Oxford University Press.

Taylor, W.L. 1953. Cloze procedure: a new tool for measuring readability. *Journalism Quarterly* 9: 206–223.

Thomas, H.C.R. and Hill, D.R. 1993. Seventeen series of graded readers. *ELT Journal* 47, 3: 250–267.

Tollefson, J. 1989. A system for improving teachers' questions. *English Teaching Forum* 27, 1: 6–9, 51.

Topping, K. 1989. Peer tutoring and paired reading: Combining two powerful techniques. *The Reading Teacher*, 42, 7: 488–494.

Upshur, J. and Turner, C. 1995. Constructing rating scales for second language tests. *ELT Journal* 49, 1: 3–12.

Urquhart, S. and Weir, C. 1998. *Reading in a Second Language: Process, Product and Practice*. Harlow: Addison Wesley Longman.

Wajnryb, R. 1988. The Dicto-gloss method of language teaching: a text-based communicative approach to grammar. *English Teaching Forum* 26, 3: 35–38.

Wajnryb, R. 1989. Dicto-gloss: a text-based communicative approach to teaching and learning grammar. *English Teaching Forum* 27, 4: 16–19.

Walker, C. 1987. Individualizing reading. *ELT Journal* 41, 1: 46–50.

Waring, R. and Takaki, M. 2003. At what rate do learners learn and retain new vocabulary from reading a graded reader? *Reading in a Foreign Language* 15, 2: 130–163.

Watson, J. 2004. Issue logs. In R.R. Day and J. Bamford (eds): 37–39.

West, M. 1941. *Learning to Read a Foreign Language*. London: Longman.

West, M. 1953. *A General Service List of English Words*. London: Longman.

West, M. 1960. *Teaching English in Difficult Circumstances*. London: Longman, Green.

West, M. 1961. Letter in Correspondence column on speed reading. *ELT Journal* 15, 3: 125–128.

Williams, R. 1986. "Top ten" principles for teaching reading. *ELT Journal* 40, 1: 42–45.

Wingfield, R.J. and Swan, D. 1971. *Situational Composition Practice*. London: Longman.

Witbeck, M.C. 1976. Peer correction procedures for intermediate and advanced ESL composition lessons. *TESOL Quarterly* 10, 3: 321–326.

Wong, P. and McNaughton, S. 1980. The effects of prior provision of context on the oral reading proficiency of a low progress reader. *New Zealand Journal of Educational Studies* 15, 2: 169–176.

Worthy, J., Moorman, M. and Turner, M. 1999. What Johnny likes to read is hard to find in school. *Reading Research Quarterly* 34, 1: 12–27.

Yano, Y., Long, M.H. and Ross, S. 1994. The effects of simplified and elaborated texts on foreign language comprehension. *Language Learning* 44, 2: 189–219.

Yopp, H.K. 1988. The validity and reliability of phonemic awareness tests. *Reading Research Quarterly* 23, 2: 159–177.

Zamel, V. 1983. The composing process of advanced ESL students. *TESOL Quarterly* 17, 2: 165–187.

Zhang, S. 1995. Re-examining the affective advantage of peer feedback in the ESL writing class. *Journal of Second Language Writing* 4, 3: 209–222.

# Index